HODDER
EDUCATION
AN HACHETTE UK COMPANY

Acknowledgements

I would like to thank the following for their comments, suggestions, typescript- and proof-reading and help in many other ways over previous editions of this book: Virginia Vinuesa Benítez, Derek and Loli Blake and their family, Mercedes Catton, Yvonne Chadwick, the late Antonio Moreno Carrascal, Susanne Elvira, José-Luis García Daza, Mike Zollo; and particularly for this fifth edition José-Luis García Daza, who has scrutinised my Spanish lists in great detail and made many useful suggestions; also my wife, Brenda, for her customary patience and encouragement.

Every effort has been made to trace all copyright holders, but if any have been inadvertently overlooked the Publishers will be pleased to make the necessary arrangements at the first opportunity.

Although every effort has been made to ensure that website addresses are correct at time of going to press, Hodder Education cannot be held responsible for the content of any website mentioned in this book. It is sometimes possible to find a relocated web page by typing in the address of the home page for a website in the URL window of your browser.

Hachette UK's policy is to use papers that are natural, renewable and recyclable products and made from wood grown in sustainable forests. The logging and manufacturing processes are expected to conform to the environmental regulations of the country of origin.

Orders: please contact Bookpoint Ltd, 130 Milton Park, Abingdon, Oxon OX14 4SB. Telephone: (44) 01235 827720. Fax: (44) 01235 400454. Lines are open 9.00–5.00, Monday to Saturday, with a 24-hour message answering service. Visit our website at www.hoddereducation.co.uk.

© Phil Turk, 1991
First published in 1991 by
Hodder Education,
An Hachette UK Company
338 Euston Road
London NW1 3BH

Second edition published 1996
Third edition published 2000
Fourth edition published 2006
This fifth edition first published 2010

Impression number   5
Year   2014 2013 2012

Cover photo © José Fuste Raga/Corbis
Typeset in Helvetica Light by Transet Ltd, Coventry, England.
Printed and bound by CPI Group (UK) Ltd, Croydon, CR0 4YY

A catalogue record for this title is available from the British Library
ISBN: 978 1444 11001 2

Introduction

This fifth edition of Palabra por Palabra has been further revised to cover a wide range of vocabulary relevant to the specifications of the main AS and A2 examination boards. Some new words and phrases have been added and some which no longer seem relevant have been discarded.

All chapters have been divided into manageable subsections, and cross-references provided where relevant vocabulary may occur in more than one chapter.

In the topic-based chapters (3 to 22), words and phrases considered more suitable for A2 level are printed in **bold**. You will notice that there are fewer of these in the earlier chapters, which mainly cover the AS topics, and that they predominate in the later chapters, which are aimed at A2 level and in some cases beyond.

At the end of each topic-based chapter you will also find a revised list of useful websites, which deal with or provide links to aspects of the particular topics.

Of the other chapters, Chapter 1 provides a vocabulary framework for developing a topic either in essay form or orally, with the more sophisticated phrases in **bold**. Chapter 2 provides material for describing character and personality, which could prove useful to a number of topics. At the end of the book, Chapter 23 deals with words which might not mean what their immediate appearance might suggest; Chapter 24 offers help in choosing the correct equivalent for English words with several meanings and offers alternatives to some overused words; and Chapter 25 offers a list of useful, mainly abstract, verbs, which you could well need, but which don't fit easily under any topic heading.

Learning vocabulary

As an advanced language student, you will by now be aware that words are the tools of the trade. However sound your knowledge of grammar and facts, and however brilliant your ideas, you cannot express them without the necessary words! And unlike when you learnt your mother tongue, unless you are extremely lucky, you won't be surrounded by people speaking Spanish 24/7! More likely your contact will be limited to a few hours of Spanish classes per week. Try, however, to increase your contact through websites, satellite broadcasts, newspapers, magazines or other materials in Spanish that you can lay your hands on. This little book provides you with a good selection of words and phrases on most of the topics you are likely to encounter, but you should also keep your own vocabulary notebook (paper or electronic) and record, as far as possible under topic headings any further ones you come across.

Vocabulary learning is a very personal process and each of us will discover the method that suits us best. However, you must accept that it won't 'stick' without some positive effort on your part. The important thing is to experiment and find the method that works best for you. And, by the way, 'method' is the key word: you must be methodical!

The following hints might help:

- Don't try to absorb too much at once: 20 words might be sufficient, possibly fewer.
- You will need to check these several times, at intervals, marking the ones you know.
- Take a break or do something else, then check again.
- Check them yet again before learning the next batch.
- Work alone, checking yourself, or get a friend or family member to test you.
- Don't let lists of words accumulate. Better to learn little and often.
- Use the words you have learnt in your written and spoken work: 'use them or lose them' applies here!

You can also expand your vocabulary by taking a word and seeing how many related words you know: e.g. *cocina* – kitchen, cooking or cooker; *cocer* – to cook; *cocción* – (process of) cooking; *cocinar* – to cook; *cocinero/a* – cook / chef. You can browse this section of a dictionary for further related words, or work with a friend to see who can find the most words. You can also see how many words you can find associated by ideas: *cocina – gas – eléctrico – electricidad – luz – alumbrar*, etc; or by opposites: *empezar – terminar, permitir – prohibir.*

Websites

A useful Spanish search engine is www.terra.es, which has a number of easily accessible links (*enlaces*). However, Google and Yahoo are perfectly adequate if you type in www.google.es or www.yahoo.es.

All the main Spanish and Spanish American press publications have their own websites, with many features relevant to the topics covered in this book. At the time of writing all allow free downloads. The main publications are:

Newspapers

El País	www.elpais.es
ABC	www.abc.es
El Mundo	www.elmundo.es
La Vanguardia	www.lavanguardia.es

Regional papers in the *Diario* series, e.g:
Diario montañés (Cantabria)   www.eldiariomontanes.es

Magazines

Cambio16	www.cambio16.info
Tiempo	www.tiempodehoy.com
¡Hola!	www.hola.com
Marca	www.marca.com
As	www.as.com

You can also find a comprehensive list of publications by visiting www.prensaescrita.com/ and adding the relevant area after the slash.

Other general websites with many useful links are the relevant Spanish government ministries:

Ministerio de Trabajo y Asuntos Sociales	www.mtas.es
Ministerio de Educación	www.mec.es
Ministerio de Industria, Turismo y Comercio	www.mityc.es
Ministerio de Ciencia y Tecnología	www.mcyt.es
Ministerio de Defensa	www.mde.es
Ministerio de Sanidad y Consumo	www.msc.es
Ministerio de Medio Ambiente y Medio Rural y Marino	www.marm.es
Ministerio de Fomento	www.fomento.es

The country suffixes for sites in Spanish-speaking countries are:

Argentina	.ar
Bolivia	.bo
Chile	.cl
Colombia	.co
Costa Rica	.cr
Cuba	.cu
Ecuador	.ec
Guatemala	.gt
México	.mx
Nicaragua	.ni
Panamá	.pa
Paraguay	.py
Perú	.pe
República Dominicana	.do
El Salvador	.sv
Spain	.es
Uruguay	.uy
Venezuela	.ve

For example, the Peruvian ministry of education site is: www.minedu.gob.pe.

You will find a list of possible websites for further research at the end of most of the topic-based chapters in this book.

¡Que te diviertas navegando!

Contents

1   **Quiero decir ...**

The purpose of this section is to provide the vocabulary to enable you to state, develop and conclude a written or spoken argument. The subsections are arranged in an order that seems to be the most logical, but do remember that many words and expressions could well be used in other parts of the argument, and in other contexts.

1.1   Preparar el terreno   *Preparing the ground*

primero	first, firstly
segundo	second, secondly
tercero	third, thirdly
el tema	subject, topic, theme
el problema	problem
la crisis	crisis
la cuestión	question (for discussion), issue
en primer / segundo / tercer lugar	in the first / second / third place
al principio	at first, at the beginning
de antemano	beforehand
tenemos que preguntarnos	we have to ask ourselves
a primera vista	at first sight
a corto plazo	in the short term
a largo plazo	In the long term
ordenar los datos	to get the facts in order
despejar el terreno	to clear the ground
¿de qué se trata?	what is it about?
resumir el tema / la cuestión	to summarise the issue
afrontar el tema / la situación	to face (up to) the issue / situation
el problema que se plantea es ...	the problem to be addressed / the problem that arises is ...
es un tema que ya lleva varios años / meses apareciendo en los medios	it's a topic which has been in the media for several years / months now
es un tema que ya me preocupa / interesa desde hace algún tiempo	it's a topic that has been concerning / interesting me for some time now
será conveniente establecer los argumentos en pro y en contra	it will be useful to establish the arguments for and against
examinar más minuciosamente los argumentos	to examine the arguments in more detail
una crisis a escala mundial	a crisis on a world scale
una situación inquietante	a worrying situation
la preocupación predominante	the main worry / concern

1.2 Aportar más ideas

Bringing in more ideas

además	besides, moreover
es más	moreover
además de lo dicho	in addition to what has been said
asimismo	likewise
en principio	in principle
en esto	at this point / stage
por consiguiente } por consecuencia	consequently, therefore
por otra parte	on the other hand
debido a esto	owing / due to this
de hecho	in fact
dicho de otro modo	in other words
dicho eso	that said, having said that
o sea ...	or to put it another way ... , or rather ...
no sólo ... sino ...	not only ... but ...
como ya se sabe	as we already know
es decir	that is to say, i.e.
en este contexto	in this context
por añadidura	in addition
a propósito	by the way
tanto ... como ...	both ... and ...
como resultado (de)	as a result (of)
resulta que ...	it turns out that ..., the result is that ...
esto explica por qué...	this explains why ...
no me explico por qué ...	I don't understand why ...
así	thus
así es que	therefore
por supuesto	of course
claro que (+ *clause*)	of course ...
en realidad	in reality, in fact
aparte de eso	apart from that
se trata de	it's a question of

1.3 Obstáculos

Obstacles

sin embargo	however
desgraciadamente } por desgracia	unfortunately
no obstante	nevertheless
a pesar de esto	in spite of this
el tropiezo	the stumbling block
sea como sea	be that as it may, that's as may be
la situación va empeorando	the situation is getting worse
teniendo en cuenta el hecho de que	bearing in mind the fact that
dado que	given that

1.4 Yo creo ...

I think ...

a mi parecer a mi modo de ver	} in my opinion
a mí me parece que ... yo opino que ...	} I think that ...
por mi parte	for my part
desde mi punto de vista	from my point of view
(no) estoy de acuerdo con los que ...	I am (not) in agreement with those who ...
estoy convencido/a de que (+ *indic*)	I am persuaded / convinced that ...
no estoy convencido/a de que (+ *subj*)	I am not persuaded / convinced that ...
esto me lleva a pensar que ...	this leads me to think that ...
que yo sepa	as far as I know
yo que tú / usted / ellos	if I were you / them
no estoy totalmente a favor de (+ *n* or *inf*)	I'm not entirely in favour of
no estoy ni a favor ni en contra de (+ *n* or *inf*)	I'm neither for nor against
tengo que confesarme en contra de (+ *n* or *inf*)	I have to admit I am against
no es una opinión / actitud que comparta yo	it's not an opinion / attitude which I share
aunque quisiera pensar de otra manera	although I would like to think otherwise
tengo que confesarme partidario/a del comentarista	I have to confess to being on the side of the commentator

1.5 Otros dicen ...

Others say ...

hay quienes dicen que ...	there are those who say that ...
la gente piensa que ...	people think that ...
otros constatan que ...	others maintain that ...
la (gran) mayoría opina que ...	the (vast) majority think that ...
según se oye / se lee	according to what one hears / reads
según una encuesta	according to a survey / opinion poll
sondear las opiniones	to sound out opinions
la verdad lisa y llana es ...	the plain truth of the matter is ...
cualquiera es capaz de ver que ...	anyone can see that ...
desde el punto de vista ajeno	from other people's point of view
es de presumir que ... según cabe presumir	} presumably
las cifras atestan que ...	the figures prove that ...
como ya se sabe	as is already known
que se sepa	as far as is known

no se puede menos de pensar que ...	one cannot help thinking that ...
es una ilusión creer que ... (+ *subj*)	we're kidding ourselves if we believe that ...
eso sería tremendamente optimista	that would be wildly optimistic
cualquiera que crea esto ...	anyone who believes this ...

1.6 La discusión sigue

The discussion continues

al contrario	on the contrary, on the other hand
visto así	seen like that
por un lado	on the one hand
por otro lado	on the other hand
de todos modos de todas maneras / formas }	in any case, anyway
en lo que concierne } en cuanto a	as for
en lugar de eso	instead of that
mientras que	whereas
no cabe duda de que ...	there is no room for doubt that ...
no se puede negar que ...	there is no denying that ...
es cierto que ...	it's certain that ...
el quid de la cuestión (es que ...)	the crux of the matter (is that ...)
hay que tener en cuenta (que ...)	you have to bear in mind (that ...)
hay que subrayar la importancia de ...	you have to emphasise the importance of ...
se tiene que hacer hincapié en ...	one has to make a special point of ... , stress ...
me limito a señalar	I confine myself to pointing out
más vale ... que ...	it's better to ... than ...
vale considerar ...	it's worth considering ...
según toda probabilidad	in all probability
nadie ignora que ...	everybody knows that ... , nobody is unaware that ...
por si acaso	just in case
no hay manera de saber si ...	there is no way of knowing whether ...
para colmo	to cap it all
y por si eso fuera poco	and as if that were not enough
no hay manera de saber si ...	there is no way of knowing whether...
a juzgar por ...	to judge by ... , judging by ...
en función de ...	in proportion to ... , according to (in that sense) ...
en razón de ...	by reason of ... , because of ... , due to ...

1.7 Por ejemplo

For example

consideremos	let's consider
pongamos por caso lo de ...	let's take for example the matter of ...
en concreto	in particular
según el caso	as the case may be
para ilustrar el problema	to illustrate the problem
con respecto a ...	with regard to ...
vamos a abordar otro aspecto	let us tackle another aspect
para considerar el asunto más detalladamente	in order to consider the matter in more detail
vamos a profundizar	let us think about it in greater depth
vale agregar que ...	it's worth adding that ...

1.8 ¿Cómo?

How?

¿hasta qué punto?	to what extent?
hasta cierto punto	to a certain extent
extremadamente	extremely
totalmente	completely, utterly
principalmente	mainly, principally
tanto más	all the more so
de cierto modo / de cierta manera / forma	in a certain way
de ningún modo / de ninguna manera	in no way
de un modo u otro / de una manera u otra	in one way or another
apenas	hardly
en ninguna circunstancia	in no circumstance(s)
simplemente / sencillamente	simply
puramente	purely, merely
prácticamente	practically, nearly
parcialmente	partially, partly
igualmente	equally, to the same extent
efectivamente	actually, in fact
parecido a ... / similar a ...	like ... , similar to ...
por la mayor parte	for the most part, mostly
a cambio de ...	in exchange for ...
sin más ni más	without further ado
se trata de saber cómo ...	it's a question of knowing how ...

1.9 ¿Cuándo?   *When?*

durante estos últimos años / meses	in the last few years / months
hace poco	a short time / while ago
anteriormente	formerly
recientemente	recently
recién construido	recently / newly built
recién nacido	recently / newly born
(recién *can be used with various past participles in this sense*)	
en el momento que ...	at the moment when ...
en aquel mismo momento	at that very moment
en un momento dado	at a given moment
hoy (en) día	nowadays
en la actualidad	nowadays, at the present time
la situación actual	the present / current situation
mientras tanto	meanwhile, in the meantime
posteriormente } con posterioridad }	subsequently, afterwards
cuanto antes } lo más pronto posible }	as soon as possible
dentro de unos pocos días	in a few days' time
dentro de poco	soon, in a short time
sin demora	without delay
algún día	some day
desde ahora	from now (on)
a partir de este / ese momento	from this / that moment (on)
a continuación	then, next, below (on page or in list)
desde ... hasta ...	from ... until ...
nunca más	never again
en la Edad Media	in the Middle Ages
en la época de la dictadura	at the time of the dictatorship
la década	decade
durante los años noventa	during the (19)90s
al final del siglo	at the turn of the century
tardar (mucho) tiempo en (+ *inf*)	to take a (very) long time in (doing)
cada cuando	every so often
cada pocos días	every few days
a cualquier hora	at any time
por primera / segunda / última vez	for the first / second / last time
por enésima vez	for the umpteenth time
cada vez (que ...)	each / every time (that ...), whenever

1.10 ¿Por qué?   *Why?*

preguntarse por qué	to wonder why
deberíamos preguntarnos si ...	we should ask ourselves if / whether ...
según los datos	according to the facts
eso explica por qué ...	that explains why ...
no me explico por qué ...	I can't explain / don't understand why ...
se trata de saber por qué ...	it's a question of knowing why ...
debemos tratar de descubrir por qué ...	we must try to find out why ...
¿para qué?	what for?, for what purpose?
para comprender mejor	in order to understand better
para que comprendamos mejor	in order / so that we can understand better
puesto que ... \} ya que ...	since / because ...
por cualquier razón	for whatever reason
la razón principal	the main reason
la piedra clave	the keystone, the keynote

1.11 La verdad es que ...   *The truth is that ...*

The expressions followed by que *in this section all express fact or assumed fact, and are therefore followed by the indicative.*

claro que es verdad que ...	of course it's true that ...
lo cierto es que ...	what is certain is that ...
no cabe duda de que ...	there's no doubt that ...
en efecto yo diría que ...	in fact I'd say that ...
quiero dejar muy claro que ...	I want to make it very clear that ...
el caso es que ...	the fact is that ...
otro factor es que ...	another factor is that ...
no se puede negar que ...	it cannot be denied that ...
queda innegable que ...	it remains / is undeniable that ...
es de suponer que ...	one presumes / supposes that ...
parece ser que ...	it seems that ...
debemos tener en cuenta que ...	we have to bear in mind that ...
si nos damos cuenta de que ...	if we realise that ...
resulta que ...	the result is / it turns out that ...
de ahí que ...	that's the reason why ...
el dilema es que ...	the dilemma is that ...
actualmente se calcula que ...	at the moment it is estimated / calculated that ...
un 70% de los entrevistados opina que ...	70% of those interviewed reckon that ...
hay quienes afirman que ...	there are those who maintain that ...
ser consciente de que...	to be conscious / aware that ...
menos mal que ...	it's a good job / thank goodness that ...

1.12 A mi juicio ...   *In my judgement ...*

When the phrase makes a judgement or indicates a purpose, the verb which follows que *is in the subjunctive. Remember that the tense of the subjunctive will depend on the rules of tense sequence, and therefore phrases containing* sería, *which is conditional, would require the imperfect subjunctive. These are marked with an asterisk (*).*

a mí me parece lógico que ...
it seems logical / sensible to me that ...

no me sorprende que ...
I'm not surprised that ...

todo esto justifica que ...
all this justifies (the fact) that ...

parece inverosímil que ...
it seems unlikely that ...

parece mentira que ...
it seems incredible that ...

a mí me resulta curioso que ...
I find it extraordinary that ...

más vale que ...
it's better / best that ...

a mí no me importa que ...
it's of no concern to me / it doesn't matter to me whether / that ...

no es porque ...
it's not because ...

¿no parece significativo que ...?
doesn't it seem significant that ...?

esto explica que se escriba así ...
that explains why it should be written like that ...

hay que asegurar que ...
one has to ensure that ...

es intolerable / insoportable que ...
it's intolerable that ...

me preocupa bastante que ...
I'm somewhat worried that ...

¿por qué tenemos que soportar que ...?
why should we put up with the fact that ... ?

sería un milagro que ...*
it would be a miracle if ...

mi preferencia sería que ...*
my preference would be that ...

¿no sería mejor que ...?*
wouldn't it be better if ...?

si no fuera porque ...*
if it weren't for the fact that ...

es de suma importancia que ...
it is of extreme importance that ...

¿por qué no exigimos todos que ...?
why don't we all demand that ...?

es de lamentar que ...
it is to be regretted that ...

es una vergüenza nacional que ...
it's a national disgrace that ...

es una afrenta a la sociedad que ...
it's an affront to society that ...

es incluso más sorprendente que ...
it's even more astonishing that ...

tiene que ser inconcebible que ...
it has to be unthinkable that ...

lo fundamental debe ser que ...
the main thing should be that ...

pongamos por caso que ...
let us suppose that ...

1.13 La validez del argumento *The validity of the argument*

razonar	to reason
el razonamiento	the reasoning
un caso irrebatible	a watertight case
un argumento de peso	a strong / robust argument
este modo de enfocar la cuestión	this approach to the question
si aceptamos este punto de vista	if we accept this point of view
el argumento no vale, porque …	the argument is no good, because …
rechazar un argumento	to reject an argument
condenar rotundamente	to condemn roundly
ver / no ver lo esencial del asunto	to see / miss the point
el argumento no está bien fundado	the argument won't hold water
no tiene pies ni cabeza	it's all at sixes and sevens
carece de sentido	it lacks sense / meaning
carece de consistencia	it lacks consistency
el punto flaco del argumento	the weak point of the argument
no tiene nada que ver con la realidad	it has nothing to do with reality
hacer la vista gorda (a)	to turn a blind eye (to)
pongamos el argumento patas arriba	let's turn the argument on its head

1.14 Soluciones y conclusiones   *Solutions and conclusions*

de acuerdo	agreed
(estar) de acuerdo con …	(to be) in agreement with
a fin de cuentas	after all, when all is said and done
en resumen	to sum up (*adv*), in brief
resumir	to sum up
la clave del problema tiene que ser	the key to the problem has to be
la solución que se destaca	the solution which stands out
tomar medidas urgentes	to take urgent measures
vuelvo a mi primera observación	I return to my first statement
ya hemos constatado que ...	we have already stated that ...
volvamos al punto de partida	let us return to the starting point
teniendo en cuenta todos los puntos de vista	bearing in mind all points of view
podemos deducir que …	we can deduce that ...
es una perspectiva …	the outlook is ...
optimista	optimistic / bright
poco optimista	not very optimistic
(muy) pesimista	(very) pessimistic / gloomy
(nada) favorable	(not very) favourable
aunque con ciertas dudas / reservas	although with certain doubts / reservations
por fin	finally, at last
en conclusión } para concluir }	in conclusion

para que la situación siga mejorando	so that the situation continues to improve
de modo que la situación no empeore	so that the situation does not deteriorate
esto nos lleva a la conclusión inevitable (que ...)	this brings us to the inevitable conclusion (that ...)
ojalá pudiera concluir diciendo que ...	I wish I could conclude by saying that ...
no hay otra conclusión que valga	there is no other valid conclusion

See also Section 24.2 for some useful hints on how to avoid overused words!

2 La gente: la personalidad y el carácter

The words and phrases in this chapter do not belong to any particular examination topic, but might be applied to any real or fictitious persons under any topic heading. You might well find them useful in describing family members in Chapter 3 and film, drama or literary characters associated with Chapter 13.

la cualidad	quality
el rasgo ⎫ la característica ⎭	feature, trait, characteristic
característico (adj) de	characteristic of
típico (de)	typical (of)
la virtud	virtue
la preferencia	preference
el estado de ánimo	mood, frame of mind
relacionarse con alguien	to relate to sb
tratar con alguien	to have dealings with sb

2.1 Las cualidades positivas *Positive qualities*

llevarse bien con alguien	to get on well with someone
tener el don de ...	to have the gift of ...
tener sentido del humor	to have a sense of humour
conservar la calma	to keep calm, keep one's cool
reflexionar antes de actuar	to think before acting
tomarse la vida tal como viene	to take life as it comes
actuar por instinto	to act instinctively
estar bien dotado de sentido común	to be well endowed with common sense
ser abierto/a	to be open, of an open disposition
ser alegre	to be happy, jolly (i.e. visibly that sort of person)
ser amigable	to be friendly
ser atento/a	to be thoughtful, kind
ser autosuficiente	to be self-sufficient
ser bondadoso/a	to be kind-hearted, generous
ser cariñoso/a	to be affectionate, loving, tender
ser cauto/a	to be cautious, wary
ser convencional	to be conventional
ser chistoso/a	to be funny, witty

ser agudo/a ⎱	to be skilful, clever
ser diestro/a ⎰	
ser exigente	to be demanding
ser autoexigente	to expect a lot of oneself
ser extrovertido/a	to be an extrovert
ser feliz	to be happy (by nature)
la felicidad	happiness
ser honrado/a	to be honest
la honradez	honesty
ser imaginativo/a	to be imaginative
ser listo/a	to be clever
estar listo/a	to be ready
ser luchador(a)	to be a fighter
ser maduro/a	to be mature
la madurez	maturity
ser optimista	to be an optimist (by nature)
estar optimista	to be optimistic (about a current matter)
ser perceptivo/a	to be perceptive
ser perfeccionista	to be a perfectionist
ser persistente	to be persistent
ser risueño/a	to be cheerful, of a sunny disposition
ser sensible	to be sensitive (NOT 'sensible')
la sensibilidad	sensitivity
ser sensato/a	to be sensible
la sensatez	good sense
ser sincero/a	to be sincere
la sinceridad	sincerity
ser tolerante	to be tolerant
la tolerancia	tolerance

2.2 Los rasgos negativos   *Negative features*

la obsesión	obsession
obsesionarse por ...	to be obsessed with ...
la fobia	phobia
no poder soportar	not to be able to stand / put up with
el defecto	defect
estar en un constante estado de :..	to be in a constant state of ...
tener tendencia a ...	to have a tendency to ...
odiar	to hate
el odio	hate, hatred
despreciar	to scorn, disdain
el desprecio	scorn, disdain
volverse irritable	to get irritable
sentirse algo inseguro/a	to feel a bit insecure
ver con malos ojos	to take a dim view of
no ver más allá de las narices	not to see further than one's nose

tener mal genio	to be bad-tempered, of an evil disposition
estar lleno/a de contradicciones	to be full of contradictions
lucirse	to show off
hacer autobombo	to blow one's own trumpet
dárselas de inteligente / deportista	to fancy oneself as intelligent / a sportsperson
ser apático/a	to be apathetic
ser asqueroso/a	to be revolting, disgusting
ser brusco/a	to be abrupt, sharp, rude
ser un canalla	to be a swine, a rotter
ser conflictivo/a	to be argumentative, quarrelsome
ser camorrista ⎫ ser chismoso/a ⎭	to be a gossip
los chismes	gossip, tittle-tattle
no ser honrado/a	to be dishonest
la falta de honradez	dishonesty
ser egoísta	to be selfish
ser emotivo/a	to be emotive, emotional
dejarse arrastrar por las emociones	to let oneself be ruled by one's emotions
ser encogido/a ⎫ ser tímido/a ⎬ ser vergonzoso/a ⎭	to be timid, shy
ser envidioso/a	to be envious
ser engreído/a	to be conceited
ser estrecho/a de miras	to be narrow-minded
ser gruñón / gruñona	to be grumpy (by nature)
ser imbécil	to be an idiot
ser indeciso/a	to be <u>indecisive</u> (by disposition)
estar indeciso/a	to be <u>undecided</u> (at this moment)
ser introvertido/a	to be an introvert
ser malévolo/a	to be malicious, spiteful
ser mezquino/a	to be mean, stingy
ser miedoso/a	to be timid, fearful
ser pesimista	to be <u>a pessimist</u> (by nature)
estar pesimista	to be <u>pessimistic</u> (about a current matter)
ser posesivo/a	to be possessive
ser rebelde	to be unruly, rebellious
ser superficial	to be superficial
ser supersticioso	to be superstitious
ser terco/a	to be stubborn, obstinate
ser testarudo/a	to be stubborn, pig-headed
ser torpe	to be clumsy, awkward, dull, dim
ser vago/a	to be slack, lazy
ser vengativo/a	to be spiteful, vindictive

3

La gente: la familia y las relaciones personales

You will know the Spanish for most of your close family members by now, but here is a reminder that when used in the masculine plural, the word often means 'one of each sex':

los padres	parents
los tíos	uncle(s) and aunt(s)
los abuelos	grandparents

los familiares	relatives
los parientes	relatives (NOT 'parents'!)
el cuñado / la cuñada	brother / sister-in-law
la nuera	daughter-in-law
el yerno	son-in-law
el hermanastro / la hermanastra	stepbrother / stepsister
el padrastro	stepfather
la madrastra	stepmother
el primo / la prima	cousin
el sobrino / la sobrina	nephew / niece
los sobrinos	nephews and nieces
el suegro / la suegra	father / mother-in-law
el árbol genealógico	family tree

3.1 Las relaciones en general

Relationships in general

hacerse amigo/a de alguien	to become somebody's friend
la amistad	friendship
entablar amistades	to strike up friendships
el desarrollo de la personalidad	the development of the personality
llevarse bien / mal con ...	to get on well / badly with ...
tener una relación especial con ...	to have a special relationship with ...
confiar en los amigos	to confide in / trust one's friends
compartir / guardar un secreto	to share / keep a secret
respetar los sentimientos ajenos	to respect other people's feelings
tolerar a los demás	to tolerate others
armar un follón	to cause a row, to kick up a fuss
sentir alegría ante el bien ajeno	to feel joy at others' wellbeing

3.2 El amor

Love

el novio / la novia	boyfriend / girlfriend, bridegroom / bride
salir con un chico / una chica	to go out with / date a boy / girl
el / la ligue (*coll*)	boyfriend / girlfriend
sentirse atraído/a por ...	to feel attracted by / to ...
enamorarse	to fall in love
estar enamorado/a (de)	to be in love (with)
el amor a primera vista ⎫ el flechazo ⎭	love at first sight
estar chiflado/a por alguien	to be crazy about sb
llevar una relación seria	to carry on a serious relationship
desarrollar una relación	to develop a relationship
el compañero / la compañera	partner
flirtear / coquetear con alguien	to flirt with sb
ligar con alguien	to chat sb up
el cariño	affection
cariñoso/a	affectionate
hacer el amor	to make love
sentir celos	to feel jealous
dar calabazas a alguien	to jilt sb
la orientación sexual	sexual orientation
del sexo opuesto	of the opposite sex
del mismo sexo	of the same sex

una relación heterosexual /
  homosexual
	a heterosexual / homosexual
	  relationship

la homosexualidad	homosexuality
el lesbianismo	lesbianism
ser gay / lesbiana	to be gay / lesbian

3.3 Vamos a casarnos

Let's get married

el prometido / la prometida	fiancé(e)
prometerse (con)	to get engaged (to)
estar prometido/a/os	to be engaged
el noviazgo	engagement
la pareja	couple
prometer	to promise
casarse (con)	to get married (to)
la boda	wedding (i.e. the ceremony)
el casamiento	wedding / marriage (ceremony or state)
el matrimonio	marriage (the state)
contraer matrimonio	to enter into matrimony / marriage
la dama de honor	bridesmaid
el padrino de boda	best man
el anillo	ring
el voto	vow

estar felizmente casados	to be happily married
ayudarse uno a otro	to help each other
el apoyo mutuo	mutual support
ser / quedarse soltero/a	to be / remain single

3.4 La familia y los niños — *Family and children*

los padres } los progenitores }	parents
estar embarazada	to be pregnant
quedar embarazada	to get pregnant
parir	to give birth (to)
el parto	birth (in sense of delivery)
nacer	to be born
el / la bebé } el nene / la nena }	baby
la criatura	baby, small child
los gemelos	twins
tienen tres críos	they've got three kids
la niñera	childminder, nanny
la baja por maternidad / paternidad	maternity / paternity leave
el cochecito de niño	pram
la sillita de ruedas	pushchair, buggy
cambiar los pañales a un bebé	to change a baby's nappy
el protector / la protectora	guardian
el / la canguro	baby-sitter
hacer / estar de canguro	to baby-sit
el hijo / la hija mayor	the elder / eldest son / daughter
el / la menor	the younger / youngest
el benjamín	the youngest son
el padrino	godfather
la madrina	godmother
los padrinos	godparents
el cumpleaños	birthday
al cumplir doce años	on reaching / when s/he turned twelve
el santo	saint's day
el bautizo	christening, baptism
bautizar	to christen, baptise
se le puso Miguel	he was named / baptised Miguel
el nombre (de pila)	name (first / Christian name)
la maternidad	maternity
la paternidad	parenthood, fatherhood
amamantar	to suckle, breastfeed
dar el pecho	to breastfeed
la cuna	cradle
mecer	to rock

criar una familia	to bring up / raise a family
la infancia	infancy
el jardín de infancia	kindergarten
la guardería (infantil)	nursery, crèche
los recuerdos de la niñez	childhood memories
la canción infantil	nursery rhyme
desde niño/a	from childhood
de niño/a	as a child
mimar a un niño	to spoil a child
una familia unida	a close family
monopolizar el cariño de los padres	to monopolise parents' affection
en el seno de la familia	in the bosom of / within the family
mostrar autoridad	to show authority
crear lazos de afecto	to create bonds of affection
evitar favoritismos	to avoid favouritism
crear un estrecho vínculo	to create a close bond
el maltrato a los niños	child abuse

3.5 La vida sexual — *Sex life*

la planificación familiar	family planning
la contracepción / anticoncepción	contraception
la píldora anticonceptiva	contraceptive pill
los métodos anticonceptivos	contraceptive methods, birth-control methods
el anticonceptivo	contraceptive
el preservativo / el condón	condom
el control de la natalidad	birth control
dejar embarazada a una mujer	to get a woman pregnant
un embarazo (no) deseado	a wanted (an unwanted) pregnancy
interrumpir el embarazo	to terminate the pregnancy
el feto	foetus
el ciclo menstrual	menstrual cycle
el aborto	abortion
abortar	to have an abortion / a miscarriage
fecundar	to fertilise
la hormona	hormone
concebir	to conceive
la fecundación *in vitro*	*in vitro* fertilisation
el niño probeta	test-tube baby
la inseminación artificial	artificial insemination
la madre portadora	surrogate mother

3.6 El divorcio

Divorce

divorciarse	to get divorced
estar divorciado/a	to be divorced
solicitar un divorcio	to apply for a divorce
la tasa de divorcio	the divorce rate
el consejero de orientación matrimonial	marriage guidance counsellor
iniciar los procedimientos del divorcio	to initiate divorce proceedings
el alejamiento	estrangement
convivir	to live together
un proceso penoso	a painful process
la ruptura matrimonial	marriage break-up
ser incompatibles	to be incompatible
cuando un matrimonio se deshace	when a marriage breaks up
la separación	separation
separarse	to become separated
perjudicar gravemente	to prejudice seriously
hijos, bienes y posesiones	children, property and possessions
el padre soltero	single father / parent (male)
la madre soltera	single mother / parent (female)
la custodia de los niños	custody of the children
el / la cónyuge	spouse
tener relaciones con	to have an affair with
la infidelidad	infidelity
volver a casarse	to remarry

3.7 La mujer

Women

el feminismo	feminism
los derechos de la mujer	women's rights
los malos tratos	ill-treatment, abuse
(no) tratar a la mujer como	(not) to treat women as
objeto sexual	sex objects
objeto de deseo	objects of desire
como si fuera algo normal	as if it were something normal
cuidar de la casa y de la familia	to look after the house and family
'en casa y con la pata quebrada'	'at home and with her leg broken' (old Spanish proverb, suggesting the woman's place is in the home – even if you have to break her leg to keep her there!)
la publicidad machista	male-orientated advertising
el papel primordial de la educación	the prime role of education

You will find vocabulary concerning women at work in Section 6.4.

3.8 La tercera edad   *Senior citizens*

jubilarse	to retire
estar jubilado/a	to be retired
los jubilados	retired people
el / la pensionista	pensioner
la persona de la tercera edad	senior citizen
la libreta de pensión	pension book
el plan de pensiones	pension scheme
la vida empieza a los 60 años	life begins at 60
el abono para la tercera edad	pensioners' travel pass
para las personas de 65 años o más } para los mayores de 65 años	for people of 65 and over
hacer lo que te dé la gana	to do as you please
el asilo de ancianos	old people's home
geriátrico/a	geriatric
estar postrado/a en cama	to be bedridden
la discapacidad	disability
el cuidador / la cuidadora	carer
el servicio de comidas a domicilio	meals on wheels
tener que depender de otros	to have to depend on others

For young people's relationships with parents, see also Section 4.2.

---

www.enbuenasmanos.com
www.mujeractual.com/familia
www.terceraedad.org

Los jóvenes

la adolescencia	adolescence
(el / la) adolescente	adolescent (n or adj)
de niño/a	as a child, when X was a child
ir creciendo	to be growing up
el comportamiento	behaviour
comportarse	to behave

4.1 Los problemas de hacerse adulto

Problems of growing up

el estado de ánimo	state of mind
estar en la edad del pavo	to be at the awkward age
estar en la edad de querer independizarse	to be of an age to want one's independence
le cuesta mucho concentrarse	s/he finds it difficult to concentrate
estar hecho/a un lío	to be all mixed up
deprimirse	to get depressed
sentirse deprimido/a	to feel depressed
el estado de depresión	state of depression
cabrearse (*coll*)	to get mad, livid
amargar	to make bitter
amargarse	to feel / become bitter
sentir amargura	to feel bitterness
sentirse amargo/a	to feel bitter
estar harto/a (de)	to be fed up (with)
hartarse (de)	to get fed up (with), weary (of)
el desarrollo de la personalidad	the development of the personality
tener problemas al relacionarse con la gente	to have problems relating to people
contar mentirijillas	to tell lies, fibs
encontrarse inseguro/a	to feel insecure
usar el argot callejero	to use street slang
hacerse el chulo	to act big / smart
superarse a sí mismo/a	to take oneself in hand, control oneself
sentir la necesidad de ser uno mismo	to feel the need to be oneself
el servicio voluntario	voluntary service
participar en las iniciativas voluntarias	to take part in voluntary initiatives

4.2 Las relaciones con los padres

Relations with parents

la autoridad	authority
las actitudes	attitudes
cuestionar la autoridad	to question / challenge authority
la autoridad paterna	parental authority
rebelarse contra la autoridad	to rebel against authority
la permisividad paterna	parental permissiveness
los padres indulgentes	lenient, tolerant parents
el castigo; castigar	punishment; to punish
las reglillas	petty rules
el comportamiento antisocial	antisocial behaviour
soltar palabrotas	to swear, use bad language
mostrarse mal educado/a	to make a show of bad manners
montar / armar un follón	to cause a row, kick up a fuss
reñir	to quarrel
ponerlo todo en tela de juicio	to question everything
llegar de madrugada	to come home in the small hours
querer salirse con la suya	to want to get one's own way
no poder entenderse con su padre / madre	to be unable to get on with one's father / mother
su madre es una antigualla	his / her mother is old-fashioned
su padre es un chapado a la antigua	his / her father is an old fuddy-duddy
estrecho/a de miras	narrow-minded
mis padres insisten en que yo (+ *subj*)	my parents insist that I ...
fastidiar a alguien	to get on someone's nerves
buscar cinco pies al gato	to make a lot of fuss over nothing, exaggerate
escuchar todos los días el mismo rollo	to hear the same old thing day after day
como si fuese lo único que importase	as if it were the only thing that mattered
no tener prejuicios	to be open-minded
compartir ideas	to share ideas
no importa quién tiene razón	it doesn't matter who's right
no es porque no lo intente	it isn't for want of trying
hacer las paces	to make it up
cada cual ofrece su opinión	each one offers his / her opinion
ponerse de acuerdo	to reach an agreement
estar de acuerdo	to be in agreement, agree

4.3 El desafecto juvenil

Disaffection of young people

un fenómeno creciente	a growing phenomenon
el desencanto	disenchantment, disillusion(ment)
la falta de oportunidades	lack of opportunities
las frustraciones	frustrations
sentirse perseguido/a y acosado/a	to feel persecuted and harassed
sentirse / estar marginado/a	to feel / be marginalised
la presión del grupo paritario	peer group pressure
no integrarse en el tejido social	to remain outside the social fabric
apurar el instante	to live for the moment
vivir el presente	to live for the present
desperdiciar la juventud	to squander one's youth
necesitar una dosis de aventura	to need a dose of adventure
romper la aplastante rutina social	to break the soul-destroying daily routine

4.4 La música pop

Pop music

la canción	song
grabar en disco	to record
la letra	lyrics, words (of a song)
el pinchadiscos	disc-jockey, DJ
la estrella de pop	pop star
la gira por Estados Unidos	US tour
el concierto	gig, concert
el festival pop	pop festival
las listas de éxitos	the charts
el disco número uno	number one hit
el sistema de amplificación	PA system
los amplificadores	loudspeakers, amplifiers
el teclado	keyboard
tocar la batería	to play the drums
los palillos	drumsticks
tocar la guitarra eléctrica	to play the electric guitar
el sintetizador	synthesiser
el / la solista	lead (singer / player)
doblar	to dub
las luces estroboscópicas	strobe lights
los focos	lights
los fans	fans

See also Section 13.4 for further vocabulary on music.

4.5 La moda   *Fashion*

una prenda de vestir	a garment, article of clothing
estrenar	to wear for the first time
la manera de vestirse	way of dressing
dar una buena imagen	to give a good image
tener un buen aspecto	to look good
expresar su personalidad en la ropa	to express one's personality in one's clothes
el diseñador / la diseñadora	designer
el modisto / la modista	fashion designer
la creación original	original creation
estar muy de moda	to be very trendy
la última moda	the latest fashion
pasar de moda	to go out of fashion
lucir un nuevo vestido	to show off a new dress
la preocupación por vestir bien	the desire to be well-dressed
saber elegir lo más elegante	to know how to choose the smartest (clothes, etc.)
saber cómo vestir	to know how to dress, have good dress sense
vestirse de una manera estrafalaria	to dress outlandishly
vestirse al estilo punk	to dress in punk style
lucir una cazadora de cuero negro	to sport a black leather jacket
los vaqueros rotos	ripped jeans
la caída de la chaqueta	the hang of a jacket
los vuelos de la falda	the spread / swirl of a skirt

You will find further vocabulary concerning young people in Chapter 5.

www.injuve.mtas.es
www.cje.org
www.cruzrojajuventud.org

5   La enseñanza

la escuela	school (usually primary)
el colegio (el cole)	state primary school, or private school for all ages up to 18
el instituto	state secondary school (12–18)
el centro	centre (often used just to denote school)
la asignatura	subject
la vuelta al cole / colegio	back / return to school
el profesor / la profesora	teacher
el / la profe (*coll*)	teacher
el maestro / la maestra	primary teacher
el castigo	punishment
castigar	to punish

5.1   La escolaridad   *The school system*

el centro docente	educational / teaching establishment
Educación Básica Obligatoria	compulsory basic education
Educación Primaria (EP)	primary education
Educación Secundaria Obligatoria (ESO)	compulsory secondary education
el módulo	module
el instituto	state secondary school (12–18)
el internado	boarding school
la academia	'crammer'
el parvulario	play school, kindergarten
un traslado de colegio	a change of school
el curso	school year
pasar de curso	to move up a year
la escolaridad	period of schooling, school system
matricularse	to sign on, to enrol (for a school)
el rendimiento escolar	school performance
las clases particulares	private classes
los métodos de enseñanza	educational / teaching methods
el folleto de información	information booklet
el temario	syllabus
las materias obligatorias	compulsory subjects
las instalaciones deportivas	sports facilities
mandar partes a casa	to send a report home
el parte de clase	school report

5.2 Tus capacidades y aptitudes

Your abilities and aptitudes

un método infalible	an infallible method
el alumno talentoso / la alumna talentosa	gifted pupil
estar bien motivado/a	to be well motivated
me falta motivación	I lack motivation
me cuesta concentrarme	I find it hard to concentrate
la capacidad de trabajo	capacity for work
tener sed de conocimientos	to have a thirst for knowledge
hacer un mayor esfuerzo	to make a greater effort
devanarse los sesos	to rack one's brains
las asignaturas que presentan mayor dificultad	the subjects which present the greatest difficulty
abordar primero las asignaturas difíciles	to tackle the difficult subjects first
las asignaturas que se pueden superar con más facilidad	the subjects which can be most easily mastered
tener aptitud para los idiomas	to have a flair for languages
no se me dan las ciencias	I'm not very good at science
ser empollón / empollona (*coll*)	to be a swot
ser curroadicto/a (*coll*)	to be a workaholic
(no) vale el esfuerzo	it's (not) worth the effort
¡ya caigo!	got it!
¡no caigo!	I don't get it!
organizar su tiempo	to organise one's time
obtener resultados	to obtain results
conocer sus deficiencias	to know one's weaknesses
la capacidad de retener conocimientos	the ability to retain knowledge
perder el hábito del estudio	to get out of the habit of studying
un sistema adecuado a las capacidades y aptitudes del alumno	a system suited to the capabilities and aptitudes of the pupil
desarrollar la capacidad autocrítica	to develop one's capacity for self-appraisal

5.3 Los problemas escolares

Problems at school

el fracaso escolar	failure at school
fracasar	to fail, to be a failure (in school)
la falta de escolaridad	lack of schooling
las expectativas de los padres / progenitores	parents' expectations
la sobreexigencia	over-expectation
flojear / ser flojo/a (en)	to be weak (at)
la escasa atención de los padres	lack of parental attention
la dislexia	dyslexia
ser disléxico/a	to be dyslexic
sufrir retraso escolar	to fall behind in one's schooling
repetir curso	to repeat a year
faltar a clase	to skip lessons
la masificación en las aulas	overcrowding in the classrooms
los materiales trasnochados	out-of-date materials
garantizar / mejorar la calidad en la enseñanza	to guarantee / improve the quality of education

5.4 Las oportunidades

Opportunities

la igualdad de oportunidades	equality of opportunities
ampliar la formación	to broaden one's education
moldear a las generaciones futuras	to shape future generations
la política educativa del gobierno	government education policy
la natalidad de los años noventa	the birth rate in the nineties
el gasto estatal en educación	state expenditure on education
proceder de las clases sociales más desfavorecidas	to come from the most disadvantaged social classes

5.5 El personal docente

Teaching staff

hacer oposiciones para profesor(a)	to apply for a teaching job (by competitive exam)
enseñar una asignatura	to teach a subject
dar clase a los alumnos	to teach pupils
el director / la directora	headteacher, principal
el pedagogo / la pedagoga	pedagogue, 'posh' word for teacher
el catedrático / la catedrática	head of department / faculty
el agregado / la agregada	assistant teacher
el / la PNN (penene) = profesor(a) no numerario/a	probationary or trainee teacher
el bedel / la bedela	caretaker, head porter
el claustro	staff meeting

las cualidades del profesor	a teacher's attributes
mantener la disciplina	to maintain discipline
relacionarse con los alumnos	to relate to one's pupils
no tener favoritismos	not to have favourites
ser capaz de motivar a los alumnos	to be capable of motivating pupils
esforzarse en hacer las clases más agradables	to try to make classes more enjoyable
autoritario/a	authoritarian
poco exigente	undemanding, lax
relajado/a	relaxed, laid back
austero/a	austere
estricto/a	strict
fomentar la discusión	to encourage discussion
reciclarse	to retrain
los profesores reclaman su valoración en la sociedad	teachers demand to be appreciated in society

5.6 Los exámenes

Examinations

la evaluación	assessment (test held several times during the school year in Spanish schools)
sacar buenas / malas notas	to get good / bad marks
sacar un sobresaliente	to get an 'excellent'
un notable	a 'very good'
un bien	a 'good'
un suficiente	a 'satisfactory'
un insuficiente	an 'unsatisfactory'
un muy deficiente	a 'very poor'
aprobar un examen por los pelos	to scrape through an exam
suspender un examen	to fail an exam
la recuperación	retake
la chuleta (*coll*)	'crib'
hacer trampas	to cheat
tener miedo a los exámenes	to have examination nerves
salir preparado/a para poder incorporarse al mercado de trabajo	to come out ready and able to join the labour market

5.7 La universidad

University

el sistema universitario	the university system
acceder a la enseñanza universitaria	to gain access to university education
ingresar en la universidad	to get into university
la solicitud de admisión	entry application
la selectividad	university entrance exams
lograr títulos	to get qualifications
el procedimiento de selección	selection procedure
cursar estudios universitarios	to follow a university course
la facultad universitaria	university faculty
el intercambio de conocimientos	exchange of knowledge
la libre circulación de las ideas	free circulation of ideas
una experiencia enriquecedora	an enriching experience
el enriquecimiento	enrichment
el desarrollo cultural	cultural development
científico	scientific development
tecnológico	technological development
la convalidación mutua de títulos	mutually agreed validation of qualifications (between countries)
las humanidades	arts, humanities
las ciencias	sciences
la licenciatura	degree
ser licenciado/a en derecho	to have a degree in law
las tasas	tuition fees
conseguir una beca	to get a grant
el préstamo gubernamental	government loan
reembolsar un préstamo	to repay a loan
estar pelado/a (*coll*)	to be hard up
estar sin blanca	to be strapped for cash, 'skint'
acumular deudas para el futuro	to pile up future debts
la tesis doctoral	doctoral thesis
la fuga de talentos	brain drain
las manifestaciones estudiantiles	student demonstrations
el líder estudiantil	student leader

---

www.mec.es
www.me.gov.ar
www.sep.gob.mx

El trabajo

el comercio	business, commerce, business studies
el director / la directora	director, manager
la ambición	ambition
la compañía / la empresa	company, firm
cobrar / ganar	to earn
la experiencia laboral	work experience
el aprendiz / la aprendiza	apprentice
el aprendizaje	apprenticeship
tomarse un año libre	to take a gap year / year off
la formación profesional	vocational training

6.1 La carrera

Career

6.1.1 Solicitar trabajo

Applying for jobs

andar en busca de empleo	to be on the lookout for a job
solicitar un puesto de trabajo	to apply for a job
el anuncio	advertisement
leer en las 'ofertas de trabajo'	to read in the 'Situations Vacant'
responder a un anuncio	to reply to an advert
la agencia de colocación	employment agency
el INEM (Instituto Nacional de Empleo)	Ministry of Employment (also equivalent of government job centre)
hacer oposiciones	to seek a job by public competition (mainly in Spanish Civil Service)
se necesita fontanero	vacancy for a plumber
un trabajo muy solicitado	a much sought-after job
la hoja de solicitud	application form
escribir una carta de solicitud	to write a letter of application
me permito dirigirme a usted para (+ *inf*)	I am writing to you in order to ...
el currículum vitæ	*curriculum vitæ*, CV
los datos personales	personal data
los títulos académicos	academic qualifications
con licenciatura en ...	with a degree in ...
la experiencia profesional	professional / work experience
pedir informes / referencias	to ask for references
dar informes / referencias	to give references, act as referee

en respuesta a su anuncio publicado en ...	in reply to your advertisement published in ...
las aficiones	interests
tengo un año de experiencia en ...	I have a year's experience in ...
aunque no tengo experiencia en ...	although I have no experience in ...
domino perfectamente el español	I have fluent Spanish
ofrecer mis servicios como ...	to offer my services as ...
la entrevista	interview
entrevistar bien	to interview well
ir bien vestido/a	to be well / smartly dressed
ser apto/a para el trabajo	to be suitable for the job
incorporarse al trabajo lo antes posible	to go out to work as soon as possible
conseguir un trabajo por enchufe	to get a job through connections, by pulling strings
estar bien enchufado/a	to have good connections, be well connected
me ofrecieron el trabajo	I was offered the job
me rechazaron	they turned me down
el rechazo	rejection, refusal
rechacé el puesto	I turned the job down

6.1.2 Las ambiciones

Ambitions

ser ambicioso/a	to be ambitious
mi única ambición es hacerme ...	my one ambition is to become a ...
le falta ambición	s/he has no ambition
buscarse una carrera en informática	to seek a career in information technology
planificar su futuro	to plan one's future
apuntar alto	to aim high
poner las miras en un puesto alto	to set one's sights on a top job
sacar adelante la carrera	to foster / advance one's career
aspirar a periodista	to have aspirations to be a journalist
prepararse para fontanero	to train as a plumber
seguir un curso de ingeniería	to follow a course in engineering
hacer un aprendizaje en carpintería	to do a carpentry apprenticeship
estudiar para abogado	to study to become a lawyer
soñar con hacerse estrella de cine	to dream of becoming a film star
trabajar de camarero	to work as a waiter
hay que promocionar la imagen	one needs to promote one's image
el potencial adquisitivo	earnings potential

6.2 El personal

Staff, personnel

un puesto de alta dirección	a senior management position
el director / la directora general	managing director
el director / la directora de ventas	sales manager
el director / la directora de personal	personnel manager
los altos cargos	top people
la oficina central	head office
el secretario / la secretaria de dirección	management secretary
el empresario / la empresaria	manager / boss
el encargado / la encargada	foreman/woman
la plantilla	staff
la mano de obra	workforce
el empleado / la empleada de banco	bank employee
el obrero / la obrera	worker
el funcionario / la funcionaria	civil servant
el empleado / la empleada	employee
el trabajador / la trabajadora	worker
el peón / la peona	unskilled worker
el peonaje	unskilled workforce, labourers
el trabajador / la trabajadora eventual	casual worker
el jornalero / la jornalera	day labourer
un trabajo de cuello blanco	a white-collar job
ser trabajador(a) autónomo/a	to be self-employed
experimentado/a	experienced
generar empleo	to generate employment
cambiar de empleo	to change jobs
la satisfacción en el trabajo	job satisfaction
el estatus	status

6.3 Las condiciones del trabajo

Working conditions

el mercado de trabajo	the labour market
la rentabilidad	profitability
la productividad	productivity
la competencia	competition
la creación de empleo	creation of employment
el contrato	contract
contratar	to contract, take on
un trabajo especializado	a specialised job
el sector de servicios	the service sector
la banca	banking

la sucursal	branch
la población obrera	the working population
el trabajo a tiempo completo	full-time work
el trabajo a tiempo parcial	part-time work
el trabajo a destajo	contract work
el trabajo con horario flexible ⎱ la flexibilización de horarios ⎰	flexitime
el trabajo por turnos	shiftwork
trabajar horas extra	to work overtime
el pluriempleo	having more than one job
asalariado	waged, salaried
el salario mínimo	minimum wage
el sueldo	pay, salary
las posibilidades de ascenso	promotion possibilities
las normas de seguridad	safety regulations
sentirse a gusto en el trabajo	to feel happy in one's work
el absentismo	absenteeism

6.4 La mujer en el trabajo — *Women at work*

la incorporación de la mujer en el trabajo	the involvement / acceptance of women at work
la discriminación sexual	sex discrimination
la igualdad de oportunidad	equality of opportunity
cobrar el 30 por ciento menos	to earn 30 per cent less
estar peor pagadas que los hombres	to be less well paid than men
pocas ocupan los altos cargos	few occupy the top jobs
el techo de cristal	the 'glass ceiling'
el acoso sexual	sexual harassment
acosar	to harass
una cuestión de actitudes	a question of attitudes
la guardería	crèche
el horario flexible	flexible hours
la baja por maternidad	maternity leave
poder diversificar su elección profesional	to be able to vary one's choice of job
tener que sacar adelante el trabajo de fuera y dentro de la casa	to have to do work outside and inside the home
la necesidad de compaginar la vida familiar con la profesional	the need to reconcile family and professional life

You will find further vocabulary on the subject of women in Section 3.7.

6.5 En la oficina   *In the office*

6.5.1 La correspondencia comercial   *Business correspondence*

Note: In business correspondence, if you are writing to or on behalf of a company, use the plural; if you are writing to a particular person representing that company, use the singular. Unless you are very well acquainted with your addressee(s) you will normally use usted / ustedes.

Muy señor mío	Dear Sir (person to person)
Muy señora mía	Dear Madam (person to person)
Muy señores nuestros	Dear Sirs (from firm to firm)
Estimado Sr. Ramírez	Dear Mr Ramírez
Estimada Sra. Blas	Dear Mrs Blas
acuso / acusamos recibo de su carta del 12 de abril	thank you for your letter of 12th April
con referencia a su pedido del 8 de mayo	with regard to your order of 8th May
en respuesta a su anuncio en El Diario	in reply to your advertisement in El Diario
tenemos el gusto de informarles que ...	we have pleasure in informing you that ...
hemos recibido una solicitud de información sobre ...	we have received a request for information about ...
le(s) agradecería / agradeceríamos nos mandara ...	I / we would be grateful if you would send us ...
tenga(n) la bondad de comunicarnos su respuesta lo antes posible	please reply as soon as possible
tenga(n) la bondad de responder por fax / correo electrónico / a vuelta de correo	please reply by fax / email / by return of post
de acuerdo con sus instrucciones	in accordance with your instructions
adjunto encontrará(n) ...	please find enclosed ...
le / la saluda atentamente	yours faithfully (from one person)
les saludan atentamente	yours faithfully (from company)

NB: If in doubt, you can just say atentamente!

remitente / rte.	sender (on back of envelope)
impresos	printed matter
certificado	registered (mail)
confidencial	confidential

6.5.2 Al teléfono

On the phone

telefonear / llamar por teléfono	to telephone
la llamada telefónica	phone call
¿me pone con la centralita?	can you put me through to the switchboard?
¿de parte de quién?	who's calling?
está(n) comunicando	the line is engaged
¿podría llamarme más tarde?	could s/he / you phone me later?

6.6 Las relaciones laborales *Labour relations*

el sindicato	trade union
el sindicalismo	trade unionism
el / la sindicalista	trade unionist
el enlace sindical	shop steward
la solidaridad de la clase obrera	working-class solidarity
el / la representante	representative
la tasa de inflación	the inflation rate
la reducción de la jornada de trabajo	reduction in the working day
exigir retribuciones mejores	to demand better remuneration
las vacaciones retribuidas / pagadas	paid holidays
el coste de la mano de obra	labour costs
el derecho a la huelga	the right to strike
ponerse en huelga ⎱ ir a la huelga ⎰	to go on strike
la comisión	committee
el convenio colectivo	collective agreement
la convocatoria	strike call
convocar manifestaciones	to call demonstrations
reivindicar	to claim, demand
la reivindicación	claim, demand
la huelga salvaje	wildcat strike
la huelga de solidaridad	sympathy strike
imponer un período de enfriamiento	to impose a cooling-off period
las negociaciones	negotiations
cuarenta horas semanales	forty-hour week
despedir por razones disciplinarias	to dismiss, sack on disciplinary grounds
negociar	to negotiate
la subida de salario	salary / wage increase

yo creo que hay otras formas de protestar y conseguir lo que se pide	I think there are other ways of protesting and achieving one's demands
la huelga es el método más eficaz con el que cuenta la gente para que la escuchen	striking is the most effective way to get people to listen to you
no se consiguió nada con la huelga	the strike achieved nothing

6.7 El paro

Unemployment

6.7.1 El sistema

The system

el paro el desempleo }	unemployment
el paro a largo plazo	long-term unemployment
las cifras / la tasa del paro / desempleo	the unemployment figures
los costes salariales	wage costs
la prestación / el subsidio	benefit
la prestación / el subsidio de paro / desempleo	dole
despedir	to sack, fire, dismiss
despedir temporalmente	to lay off
el despido	redundancy
la compensación por despido	redundancy pay
la reducción de la plantilla	reduction in staff
reducir la plantilla sin despedir	to reduce staff by natural wastage
obligar a una persona a que se jubile anticipadamente	to force someone into early retirement

6.7.2 Las consecuencias

The consequences

estar parado/a, desempleado/a	to be unemployed
los parados / desempleados	the unemployed
incorporarse a las colas de los parados	to join the dole queues
sentirse rechazado/a	to feel rejected
sentir que uno no vale nada	to feel worthless
los resultados psicológicos de estar parado/a	the psychological results of being unemployed
ser una estadística	to be a statistic

reciclar a alguien	to retrain sb
reciclarse	to retrain (i.e. to get retrained)
el reciclaje	retraining
dimitir	to resign, take voluntary redundancy
jubilarse	to retire
adaptarse a los cambios	to adapt to changes
acostumbrarse a los cambios tecnológicos	to get used to technological changes

www.redtrabaja.es
www.mtas.es/mujer

El ocio

la actividad	activity
el aficionado	fan
el atletismo	athletics
el baile	dance
bailar	to dance
el baloncesto	basketball
el boxeo	boxing
el / la cantante	singer
la ciencia-ficción	science fiction
el concierto	concert
la corrida de toros	bullfight
el deporte	sport
el / la deportista	sportsman/woman
deportivo/a	sports (adj), sporting
la diversión	entertainment, amusement
divertirse	to enjoy oneself
¡que te diviertas!	enjoy yourself, have a good time!
la entrada	(entry) ticket
el equipo	team
el espectáculo	show
el esquí	ski, skiing
esquiar	to ski
el estadio	stadium
la función	function
el hobby	hobby
el interés	interest
el jugador / la jugadora	player
nadar	to swim
la natación	swimming
participar (en)	to take part (in)
el partido	game, match
el pasatiempo	hobby, pastime
el polideportivo	sports centre
los ratos libres ⎫ el tiempo libre ⎭	free / spare time
la sala de fiestas	hall
la taquilla	box office
tocar un instrumento	to play an instrument
el videojuego	videogame

7.1 Los deportes   *Sports*

las actividades lúdicas	recreational activities
ser deportista	to be keen on sport
las instalaciones deportivas	sports facilities
la selección	team (selection)
la plantilla	squad
la junta directiva	management committee
los seleccionadores	the selectors
el liderazgo	leadership
el entrenador / la entrenadora	trainer
entrenarse	to train
el adversario / la adversaria	opponent
el árbitro / la árbitra	referee, umpire
el terreno de juego	the field of play
el vestuario	changing room
el campeonato	championship
el campeonato mundial	world championship
la liga	league
la copa	cup
el trofeo	trophy
derrotar	to defeat
la derrota	defeat
permanecer imbatido/a	to remain unbeaten
la competición	competition (contest or act of competing)
los deportes competitivos	competitive sports
el concurso	competition (= contest)
la competencia	competition (= competitiveness)
el deporte de equipo	team sport
el equipo rival	rival team
el vencedor / la vencedora	winner
el resultado	result
patrocinar	to sponsor
el patrocinador / la patrocinadora	sponsor
el grupo patrocinador	sponsoring group
el patrocinio	sponsorship
tomar la iniciativa	to take the initiative
jugar bien bajo presión	to play well under pressure
el espíritu de rivalidad	rivalry, competitive spirit
fomentar el espíritu del equipo	to foster team spirit
proveer ejercicio físico	to provide physical exercise
mantenerse en forma	to keep fit
la sensación de bienestar	feeling of wellbeing
quemar grasas	to burn off fat
reducir el estrés	to reduce stress
aumentar la calidad de vida	to increase the quality of life

7.1.1 El fútbol y el rugby

Football and rugby

la temporada de fútbol	football season
el abono de temporada	season ticket
los delanteros	forwards
los defensores	defence
el ariete	striker
el enfrentamiento	encounter, confrontation
la fase final del campeonato	the final phase of the championship
marcar un gol	to score a goal
lograr el primer gol	to achieve the first goal
hacer circular el balón	to pass the ball around
chutar	to shoot
la mano	handball (i.e. touching with hand)
oeder un penalti	to give away a penalty
la quiniela (futbolística)	football pools
el boleto	pools form
el ensayo	try
el drop	drop goal
transformar	to convert
las competiciones europeas	European competitions
el partido tendrá lugar	the match will take place
el torneo	tournament
marcar un ensayo	to score a try
ganar cinco puntos	to win / score five points
¿cómo van?	what's the score? (game in progress)
¿cuál es el resultado?	what's the (final) score / result?
el Real Madrid batió al Barcelona de dos a uno	Real Madrid beat Barcelona 2–1
empatar con	to draw with
el resultado fue empate cero a cero	the result / score was a nil-nil draw

7.1.2 El atletismo

Athletics

el / la atleta	athlete
el corredor / la corredora	runner, competitor, athlete
batir el récord	to beat the record
la carrera	race
los cien metros lisos	the hundred metres flat
el maratón	marathon
el salto de longitud / de altura	long / high jump
los Juegos Olímpicos	Olympic Games
la Olimpiada	Olympiad
el estadio olímpico	Olympic stadium
conseguir una medalla de oro / plata / bronce	to get a gold / silver / bronze medal
la ciudad anfitriona	host city
las pruebas	trials

el tenis	tennis
el golpe	shot
el revés	backhand
la volea	volley
el saque	service
la pista de tenis	tennis court
pasarse los sábados en el campo de golf	to spend one's Saturdays on the golf course
el patinaje sobre hielo	ice skating
la pista de patinaje	skating rink
el campeón / la campeona internacional sobre hielo	international ice champion
el patinaje artístico	figure skating
entusiasmarse por el esquí	to be mad on skiing
las pistas de esquí	ski slopes
dedicarse al ciclismo	to do a lot of cycling
la vuelta a España	cycle race around Spain, *tour d'Espagne*
las carreras de caballos	horse racing
el hipódromo	racecourse
apostar	to bet
jugarse el dinero	to gamble
el juego de azar	game of chance
cazar	to hunt, shoot
ir de caza	to go hunting / shooting
los deportes de alto riesgo	high-risk sports
bucear	to skin-dive
el buceo	skin-diving
el buceador / la buceadora	skin-diver
el traje isotérmico	wetsuit
el vuelo libre	hang gliding
el ala (*f*) delta	hang glider
el ultraligero	microlight
despegar	to take off
aterrizar	to land
la pista de aterrizaje	runway, landing strip
pertenecer a un club de deportes acuáticos	to belong to a water-sports club
acceder a un cursillo de iniciación	to go on a beginner's course
el senderismo	hiking, trekking
salir de excursión	to go on a trip
la ornitología	ornithology, bird watching
ser amante del aire libre	to be fond of the fresh air
costearse el equipo	to afford the equipment
los gastos de mantenimiento	maintenance costs

7.2 Juegos y pasatiempos de salón   *Indoor games and pastimes*

un pasatiempo terapéutico	a therapeutic pastime
dedicarse al coleccionismo	to go in for collecting
coleccionar sellos / monedas	to collect stamps / coins
ampliar su colección	to expand one's collection
reunir antigüedades	to collect antiques
el afán de guardar	the urge to hoard things
atesorar	to treasure
tener valor sentimental / como curiosidad	to have sentimental / curiosity value
ir haciéndose con objetos	to go on acquiring things
tener una auténtica pasión de coleccionista	to have a real passion for collecting
la obra de arte	work of art
la tienda especializada	specialist shop
sacar fotos / fotografías	to take photos
revelar un rollo de película	to develop a roll of film
la cámara digital	digital camera
la tarjeta de memoria	memory card
imprimir	to print
rechazar	to reject
borrar	to erase
una partida de ajedrez	a game of chess
la tabla / pieza de ajedroz	chess board / piece
dar mate (a alguien)	to checkmate (sb)
asistir a una clase nocturna	to go to an evening class
empezar con el español	to take up Spanish

7.3 La comida y la bebida   *Eating and drinking*

7.3.1 Comer   *Eating*

la cocina española	Spanish cooking
ser cocinero/a experto/a	to be an expert cook
los comestibles	foodstuffs
saborear un plato	to savour, taste a dish
saber a ajo	to taste of garlic
picante	hot (spicy)
el menú gastronómico	gourmet menu
el menú turístico	cheap, set menu
el plato combinado	set main course
ser goloso/a	to have a sweet tooth
ser glotón / glotona	to be a glutton
salir a un restaurante	to eat out
el restaurante de cinco tenedores	'five fork' (= luxury) restaurant

tomarse unos pinchos / unas tapas	to have some tapas
ofrecer un ambiente acogedor	to offer a friendly atmosphere
no es un restaurante cualquiera	it's not any old restaurant
se come bien ahí	the food's good there
la comida rápida	fast food
la hamburguesería	burger bar

7.3.2 Beber — *Drinking*

vamos a tomar algo	let's have a drink
el refresco	soft drink
la bodega	wine bar
la denominación de origen	mark of origin (of wine)
el vino corriente / el peleón	ordinary wine, 'plonk'
la fiesta	party
el club nocturno	nightclub
la juerga	binge
emborracharse	to get drunk
estar borracho/a como una cuba	to be as drunk as a lord
ser un borracho / una borracha	to be a drunkard
cogerse una borrachera	to go on a drinking binge
la litrona	one-litre bottle of beer
hacer un botellón	to drink a lot of alcohol in public places, to go binge drinking
ir de bares	to go on a pub-crawl
la resaca	hangover
abstenerse	to abstain
abstenerse del alcohol ⎫ ser abstemio/a ⎭	to be teetotal
las bebidas sin alcohol	non-alcoholic drinks
someter a la prueba del alcoholímetro	to breathalyse

7.4 No hacer nada — *Doing nothing*

no hacer nada en absoluto	to do nothing whatsoever
echarse una siestecita	to have forty winks / a snooze
no mover un dedo para ayudar en la cocina	not to lift a finger to help in the kitchen
quedarse pegado/a al televisor	to be glued to the television
pasarse los ratos libres escuchando CDs / su MP3	to spend one's free time listening to CDs / one's MP3
el haragán / la haragana de sofá	couch potato
haraganear	to idle / lounge around
soñar despierto/a	to daydream
tumbarse al sol	to lie in the sun

You will find further leisure activities in Section 9.3.4 and Chapter 13.

http://es.sports.yahoo.com
www.marca.es
www.guiadelocio.com
www.ociototal.com

La vida urbana

la acera	pavement
las afueras	suburbs, outskirts
aparcar	to park
el aparcamiento	car park
la avenida	avenue
el barrio	district, suburb
la calle	street
céntrico/a	central
el centro comercial	shopping centre / mall
concurrido/a	busy (crowded)
la fábrica	factory
el / la habitante	inhabitant
la zona	district, area

8.1 La administración y los habitantes

Administration and inhabitants

el ciudadano / la ciudadana	citizen, town dweller
el madrileño / la madrileña	citizen of Madrid
el barcelonés / la barcelonesa	citizen of Barcelona
el sevillano / la sevillana	citizen of Seville
el ambiente	ambience, atmosphere
la capital administrativa	administrative capital
la capital económica	economic capital
el municipio	town, municipality, town council
el Ayuntamiento	town hall, town council
el concejo	council
el concejal / la concejala municipal	town councillor
la Diputación	equivalent of District Council
el presupuesto comunitario	the community budget
la urbanización	urban development
la planificación urbana	town planning
la persona que viaja diariamente al lugar de trabajo	commuter
viajar diariamente al trabajo	to commute to work

8.2 La infraestructura   *Infrastructure*

el casco histórico	historic centre
el barrio antiguo	old quarter
el paso elevado	flyover
el paso subterráneo	underpass
la peatonalización	pedestrianisation
la zona peatonal	pedestrian area
la autopista elevada	elevated motorway
la autovía	dual carriageway
la glorieta	roundabout
la carretera de circunvalación	ring road
la necesidad de más variantes	the need for more bypasses
la calle de dirección única	one-way street
la dirección prohibida	wrong way (e.g. in one-way street)
la desviación	diversion
el carril bus	bus lane
el cruce de peatones	pedestrian crossing
la pista / el carril para ciclistas	cycle track / lane
la remodelación del centro	redevelopment / restructuring of city centre
la vigilancia policial	police patrol
una solución al tráfico de Madrid	a solution for the Madrid traffic

8.3 Vivir en la ciudad   *Living in town*

8.3.1 La vivienda   *Housing*

las condiciones de vida	living conditions
la aglomeración	conurbation
la ciudad dormitorio	dormitory town
la vecindad	neighbourhood
los vecinos	neighbours, inhabitants
la manzana	block (of buildings)
el inmueble de lujo	luxury property
el rascacielos	skyscraper
el chalé independiente	detached house
la agencia inmobiliaria	estate agent's
el piso piloto	show flat
el bloque de pisos	block of flats
con cocina amueblada	with a fitted kitchen
el propietario / la propietaria	owner, proprietor
el inquilino / la inquilina	tenant
el domicilio	address, home

una casa de alquiler	a rented house
alquilar un piso	to rent a flat
arrendar	to rent
deber el alquiler	to owe the rent
la vivienda	dwelling
la hipoteca	mortgage
hipotecar	to mortgage
la vivienda unifamiliar	one-family dwelling / unit
la casucha	hovel
la chabola	hovel, shanty
el barrio de chabolas	shanty town
los sin techo	homeless people
dormir a la intemperie	to sleep rough
el barrio desfavorecido	run-down district
el espacio verde	green space
la residencia secundaria	second home
el polígono residencial	residential development, estate
dar prioridad a la estética	to give priority to aesthetic considerations
el solar de construcción	building site
modernizar	to modernise
reparar	to repair
derribar / derrumbar	to demolish, pull down
derribarse / derrumbarse	to collapse
descuidar un edificio	to neglect a building
descuidado	run-down
en las afueras	on the outskirts / in the suburbs
en el casco urbano	in the city centre
el almacén	store (shop or warehouse)
la gran superficie ⎫ el hipermercado ⎭	hypermarket
los grandes almacenes	department store(s)
la zona industrial	industrial zone / park
el polígono industrial	industrial estate
la oferta de viviendas disponibles	building stock
la escasez de viviendas	housing shortage
la necesidad de viviendas	housing needs
el programa de vivienda	housing programme
la escasez de viviendas de alquiler	shortage of rented property

8.3.2 Las ventajas de vivir en la ciudad

Advantages of living in a town

renunciar al coche	to give up the car
poder aprovechar los transportes públicos	to be able to make use of public transport
gastar menos dinero en los transportes	to spend less money on transport
el abono	travel card
el descuento	discount
el usuario de los autobuses	bus user
tenerlo todo al alcance	to have everything within reach
ir en bici(cleta)	to go by bike / bicycle
ir andando a las tiendas	to walk to the shops
una buena gama de diversiones	a good range of entertainments
la movida nocturna	nightlife
la posibilidad de mejor atención médica	possibility of better medical attention

8.3.3 Los inconvenientes

Disadvantages

la(s) hora(s) punta	rush hour, peak time
los autobuses van hasta los topes	the buses are packed
el caos del tráfico	traffic chaos
el atasco	traffic hold-up
atascarse	to be held up
el embotellamiento	traffic jam, bottleneck
agravar el problema del tráfico	to worsen the traffic problem
el tráfico es desesperante	the traffic is impossible
la polución / la contaminación	pollution
polucionar / contaminar	to pollute / contaminate
el ruido infernal	infernal noise
el humo de los tubos de escape	exhaust fumes
emitir gases nocivos	to emit noxious fumes
causar problemas respiratorios	to cause respiratory problems
hacer estragos con la salud	to wreak havoc with one's health
el aparcamiento subterráneo	underground car park
no se puede estacionar / aparcar	you can't park
estacionamiento prohibido	no parking
el / la guardia de tráfico	traffic policeman/woman, traffic warden
cerrado por obras	closed for roadworks
la grúa	crane (to tow away cars)
remolcar	to tow (away)
el cepo	wheelclamp

8.4 La seguridad ciudadana

Law and order

8.4.1 Problemas y causas

Problems and causes

la inseguridad ciudadana	citizens' feeling of insecurity / decline in law and order
el crimen (*pl* crímenes)	crime (in general or particular)
el delito	crime, offence (particular)
el ladrón / la ladrona	thief, robber, burglar
escalar una casa	to burgle / break into a house
el escalamiento	burglary, break-in
robar	to steal
el robo ⎫ el hurto ⎭	theft
el asesinato / el homicidio	murder
asesinar	to murder
el asesino ⎫ el / la homicida ⎭	murderer
la pena de muerte	death penalty
el atraco	assault, mugging
atracar	to assault, mug
la agresividad	aggressiveness
la pandilla (callejera)	(street) gang
la tribu	tribe
la guerra tribal	tribal warfare, gang warfare
asumir una actitud provocativa	to adopt a provocative attitude
la crispación	tension
destrozarlo todo	to smash everything up
los enfrentamientos	confrontations
el drogadicto / la drogadicta	drug addict
la drogodelincuencia	drug-addicted crime
(bajo) los efectos del alcohol o de la droga	(under) the influence of drink or drugs
entonarse	to get high
lanzar improperios	to hurl abuse
las luchas callejeras	street fights
montar bronca (*coll*)	to cause a riot / row / scrap
no soportar el aspecto de alguien	not to be able to stand someone's appearance
la violencia futbolística	football violence
una orgía de violencia	an orgy of violence
desatar la violencia	to unleash violence
mendigar	to beg
el mendigo / la mendiga	beggar
la mendicidad	begging
el vagabundo	tramp
el ocupa	squatter

la privación urbana	urban deprivation
los problemas de los barrios céntricos	inner-city problems
no se puede soportar este modo de comportarse	we can't put up with this sort of behaviour
a mí no me extraña que haya tanta violencia	I'm not surprised that there's so much violence

8.4.2 Remedios y sanciones

Solutions and sanctions

la seguridad ciudadana	law and order, public safety
mantener el orden público	to keep law and order
la policía	police (force)
la Guardia Civil	Civil Guard, (crime) police
el / la guardia	policeman/woman
la protección policial	police protection
aumentar las patrullas policiales	to increase the number of police patrols
el coche-patrulla	police car
estar de ronda	to be on the beat
la policía de barrio	neighbourhood police
el castigo / castigar	punishment / to punish
la cárcel / encarcelar	prison / to imprison
la multa / multar	fine / to fine
los vigilantes	vigilantes
la autodefensa	self-defence
la vigilancia vecinal	neighbourhood watch
mejorar el alumbramiento público	to improve street lighting
la farola	street light
acorralar	to confine, 'kettle'
la prohibición de vender alcohol	ban on the sale of alcohol
un problema con pocas vías de solución	an almost insoluble problem

You will find further vocabulary on the subject of transport in Chapter 10, and on the environment in Chapter 14.

www.dgt.es
www.mviv.es
www.madrid.org

La vida rural

9.1 La tierra
The land

el campo	the country (as opposed to town) / arable field
el campesino / la campesina	peasant, countryman/woman
el terreno	plot
tener 20 hectáreas de terreno	to have 20 hectares of land
la parcela	small plot, strip of land
parcelar	to divide into small plots
depender de la agricultura	to depend on agriculture
no se puede vivir de la tierra	you can't live off the land
la huerta	market garden
la finca	property, country estate
la granja	farm (usually small, in northern Spain)
la dehesa	pasture, meadow
el cortijo	farm, estate (especially in Andalucía)
el minifundio	smallholding, small farm
el latifundio	large estate
el minifundista	smallholder
el latifundista	owner of large estate
el minifundismo / latifundismo	ownership corresponding to the above, often with reference to problems caused by the respective systems
el terrateniente ausente	absentee landlord
heredar una parcela	to inherit a plot
la reforma agraria	agrarian / land reform
integrarse en una cooperativa	to join / form a cooperative
convertirse en ciudad dormitorio	to become a dormitory town

9.2 La agricultura
Agriculture

9.2.1 La labranza de la tierra
Working the land

el agricultor / la agricultora	farmer
la zona agrícola	agricultural / farming area
el pueblo agrícola	farming village
arable	arable
cultivar patatas	to grow potatoes
los cultivos	crops
los productos	produce, crops

el cultivo de naranjas	orange growing
el cultivador / la cultivadora de aceitunas	olive grower
el aceitunero / la aceitunera	olive picker
la recolección de la aceituna	olive gathering
la cosecha	harvest, crop
la cosechadora	combine harvester
cosechar a máquina	to harvest by machine
la mecanización de la agricultura	mechanisation of agriculture
coger a mano	to pick by hand
segar	to reap
la siega	reaping
arar la tierra	to plough (up) the land
el arado	plough
el surco	furrow
germinar	to germinate
irrigar	to irrigate
regar	to water, irrigate
la acequia	irrigation channel
el desagüe	drain, outlet
los cereales	cereals
sembrar trigo	to sow wheat

NB: *Rather than use a general word for 'field' such as* campo, *Spanish often adds* -al *to the crop grown, hence:*

el trigo / el trigal	wheat / wheat field
el maíz / el maizal	maize / maize field
la cebada / el cebadal	barley / barley field
el arroz / el arrozal	rice / rice field, paddy field
la berza / el berzal	cabbage / cabbage field, etc.
la naranja / el naranjal	orange / orange grove

Note also:

la cañavera / el cañaveral	reed grass / reed grass bed(s) (*Cabo Cañaveral* is 'Cape Canaveral', where the USA launches its space vessels!)
el olivo	olive tree
el olivar	olive grove
las verduras	greens, vegetables
las hortalizas	vegetables, garden produce
la necesidad de modernizar la agricultura	the need to modernise agriculture
el programa de modernización agrícola	agricultural modernisation programme
el invernadero	greenhouse
cultivar bajo plástico	to grow under plastic
crear un mar de plástico	to create a sea of plastic
el cultivo orgánico	organic farming

favorecer abonos químicos / orgánicos	to favour chemical / organic fertilisers
los nitratos calan la tierra	nitrates soak into the soil
el estiércol	manure
la tierra baldía	sterile, waste land
dejar en barbecho	to leave fallow, set aside
la subvención agrícola	farm subsidy
la Política Agraria Común (PAC)	Common Agricultural Policy (CAP)

9.2.2 La cría del ganado y otros animales

Rearing cattle and other animals

la ganadería la industria ganadera }	stockbreeding, cattle raising, cattle farming
el ganado	stock, livestock
el ganadero / la ganadera	stockbreeder, cattle raiser
la feria de ganado	cattle fair
el novillo	bullock, steer
el vaquero	herdsman, cowman
el prado / la pradera	meadow, grazing land
pastar las vacas	to graze cows
tener 50 reses	to have 50 head of cattle
la industria lechera	dairy farming
el ganado lechero	dairy herd
ordeñar las vacas	to milk cows
el ordeño	milking
el establo	cowshed
el corral	farmyard
el rebaño de ovejas / cabras	flock of sheep / goats
el pastor	shepherd
la cuota para la producción de la leche	milk (production) quota
los productos lácteos	dairy produce
el mal / la enfermedad de la vaca loca	mad cow disease
la trashumancia	transhumance (seasonal movement of cattle to new pastures: it still happens!)
el prado	meadow, pasture
la cría de cerdos	pig breeding
los piensos	fodder

9.2.3 La industria vinícola

The wine industry

la vid	vine
la viña / el viñedo	vineyard
la cooperativa vinícola	wine cooperative
la vendimia	grape harvest
la bodega	wine-producing establishment
la vinicultura	wine production
vinificar	to produce wine
la región vinícola	wine-producing area
embotellar	to bottle
el embotellamiento	bottling

9.3 Vivir en el campo

Living in the country

9.3.1 Las ventajas

Advantages

respirar aire puro	to breathe pure air
disfrutar el paisaje	to enjoy the scenery
dejar atrás el bullicio de la ciudad	to leave the bustle of the city behind
aprovechar la paz y tranquilidad	to enjoy the peace and quiet
vivir en armonía con la naturaleza	to live in harmony with nature
buscarse una vida tranquila	to seek a quiet life
la gente tiene tiempo para hablar	people have time to talk
despertarse con el canto de los pájaros	to wake up to bird song
encontrar la casita de sus sueños en el campo	to find one's dream cottage in the country
aislarse en lo más hondo del campo	to cut oneself off in the depths of the countryside

9.3.2 Los inconvenientes

Disadvantages

la necesidad de mejorar la red de carreteras	the need to improve the road network
se llega por una carretera estrecha y tortuosa	you get to it along a narrow, winding road
lleno/a de baches	full of potholes
la falta de servicios	the lack of services
la falta de transportes públicos	lack of public transport
la supresión de las líneas de autobús / tren	closure of bus / train routes
se tarda bastante en llegar a la ciudad	it takes quite a long time to get into town
vivir en un pueblo aislado	to live in a remote village
en caso de emergencia	in an emergency
cortar el suministro de agua / electricidad	to cut off water / electricity supplies

no estás seguro/a de que tengas la mejor atención médica	you're not sure of getting the best medical attention
los chismes del pueblo	village gossip
el '¿qué dirán?'	what will the neighbours say?
meter la nariz en las vidas ajenas	to poke one's nose into other people's business
el ambiente opresivo de la vida del pueblo	the oppressive atmosphere of village life

9.3.3 Los cambios demográficos *Demographic changes*

el éxodo rural	the rural exodus
la emigración	emigration, migration (from place of origin, not necessarily to or from abroad)
emigrar	to emigrate
los trabajadores extranjeros	foreign workforce
marcharse a América / Barcelona	to go off to America / Barcelona
la falta de trabajo y oportunidades	lack of work and opportunities
con la esperanza de ganar más fuera	in the hope of earning more elsewhere
cobrar más en el extranjero	to earn more abroad
buscarse una mejora del nivel de vida	to look for an improvement in one's standard of living
desarraigarse	to uproot oneself
ser incapaz de adaptarse	to be unable to adapt
volver al lugar de origen	to return to where you came from
diversificar	to diversify
fomentar el desarrollo del turismo	to encourage the development of tourism
incrementar la capacidad turística	to increase the tourist capacity
alquilar habitaciones	to let rooms

9.3.4 Los pasatiempos campestres *Country pursuits*

la caza	hunting / shooting
cazar	to hunt / shoot (an animal)
el coto de caza	game reserve
la caza de la perdiz	partridge shooting
la caza del zorro	foxhunting
los perros (de caza)	hounds
cazar ciervos	to go stag hunting
el cazador / la cazadora	huntsman/woman
el cazador furtivo	poacher
el faisán	pheasant
el jabalí	wild boar

la escopeta	shotgun
disparar a un conejo	to shoot at a rabbit
matar un conejo a tiros	to shoot a rabbit (dead)
estar en pro / a favor de la caza	to be for / in favour of hunting
los derechos de los animales	animal rights
el / la activista de derechos de animales	animal rights activist
el deporte en que se mata a un animal	blood sport
estar en contra de los deportes crueles	to be against cruel sports
abatir un ave	to shoot / bring down a bird
la perdigonada	lead shot
despedazar la presa	to tear the quarry to pieces
hay que preguntarse si la caza es cruel o no lo es	you have to ask yourself whether hunting is cruel or not
la matanza selectiva de focas	seal culling
ADDA / la Asociación para la Defensa de los Derechos de los Animales	Association for the Defence of Animal Rights
la pesca	fishing, angling
pescar	to fish
la caña de pesca	fishing rod
el anzuelo	hook
el cebo	bait
la pesca de la trucha	trout fishing
pasar horas a orillas del río	to spend hours on the river bank
el coto de pesca	fishing reserve
el caballo	horse
la yegua	mare
la caballeriza	stable, stud, horse-breeding establishment
la equitación	horse riding
ir / montar a caballo	to ride a horse, go horse-riding
la romería	pilgrimage, procession (usually to a local shrine)
el santuario	shrine (to a local saint or the Virgin Mary)

www.marm.es

10 Los transportes, el turismo y las vacaciones

la carretera	road
el camino	track, lane
la autopista	motorway
la autovía	dual carriageway
el ferrocarril	railway
la estación de ferrocarriles	railway station
la estación de autobuses	bus station

10.1 Las redes de transporte *Transport networks*

10.1.1 Los ferrocarriles

Railways

La RENFE (Red Nacional de los Ferrocarriles Españoles)	Spanish Railways
FEVE (Ferrocarriles Españoles de Via Estrecha)	company which runs Spanish narrow gauge lines
el AVE (Alta Velocidad Española) (*f*)	Spanish high-speed train
el tren de alta velocidad	high-speed train
el transporte ferroviario	rail transport, transport by rail
la red española de ferrocarriles	the Spanish railway network
el ancho de vía (inter)nacional	the (inter)national gauge
la locomotora de gran potencia	high-powered locomotive
una velocidad superior a 200 kilómetros por hora	a speed above 200km per hour
el tren de largo recorrido	long-distance train
el tren de cercanías	suburban train
el transporte de mercancías	freight transport
modernizar el sistema	to modernise the system
ampliar la red del Metro	to extend the Underground network
construir nuevas líneas	to build new lines
conseguir un mayor número de pasajeros / de mercancías en los trenes	to attract more passengers / goods to use the trains
tener trenes eficaces y competitivos	to have an efficient and competitive train service
atraer más comercio de las carreteras	to attract more business away from the roads
reducir las tarifas	to reduce fares
quitar trenes	to cut train services

el único medio de transporte público	the only means of public transport
la privatización / nacionalización de los ferrocarriles	privatisation / nationalisation of the railways
es cuestión de rentabilidad	it's a question of profitability
incrementar la inversión	to increase investment
eliminar las líneas no rentables	to close down unprofitable lines

10.1.2 Las carreteras

Roads

la línea de autobús	bus route
mejorar el servicio de autobuses	to improve the bus service
mejorar el horario	to improve the timetable
llegar / salir a intervalos regulares	to arrive / depart at regular intervals
los autobuses siempre van atestados	the buses are always full
el abono de transportes semanal / mensual	weekly / monthly travel card
el carril bus	bus lane
el transporte pasajero rápido	rapid passenger transport
reintroducir los tranvías eléctricos	to reintroduce electric trams
la calzada	roadway
el cruce peligroso	dangerous junction / crossroads
el punto negro	(accident) black spot
la velocidad excesiva	excessive speed
la infraestructura	infrastructure
la seguridad	safety
la carretera de peaje	toll road
el desplazamiento	movement (from one place to another)
desplazarse	to travel, move about
el tráfico de largo recorrido	long-distance traffic
el volumen de tráfico	volume of traffic
planificar la red de carreteras	to plan the road network
el programa de construcción de carreteras	road-building programme
el factor más importante en la planificación de las carreteras	the most important factor in road planning
abrir un nuevo tramo	to open a new section (of road)
evitar daño medioambiental	to avoid environmental damage
cometer un atropello ecológico	to commit an ecological outrage
el coste medioambiental	the environmental cost
incrementar los impuestos sobre la gasolina	to increase tax on petrol
la falta de dinero para pagar la infraestructura	the lack of money to pay for the infrastructure

10.1.3 El transporte aéreo

Air transport

la línea aérea	airline
la línea aérea de bajo precio	low-cost / budget airline
el vuelo chárter	charter flight
el vuelo regular	scheduled flight
el jumbo	jumbo jet
facturar el equipaje	to check in
el límite de equipaje	baggage allowance
el control de seguridad	security check
la seguridad aérea	air safety, safety in the air
el registro de equipaje	baggage search
radiografiar	to X-ray
las horas perdidas en el aeropuerto	hours wasted in the airport
la necesidad / lata de las prolongadas precauciones de seguridad	the need for / nuisance of prolonged safety precautions
hay que tener paciencia	you have to be patient
impacientarse	to get impatient
el retraso	delay
el desfase horario	jet lag
la diferencia de horario	time difference
emitir x toneladas de dióxido de carbono	to emit x tons of carbon dioxide
estrellarse con la pérdida de 300 vidas	to crash with the loss of 300 lives
el siniestro	disaster
la catástrofe	catastrophe, disaster
el fallo mecánico	mechanical fault
desplomarse del cielo	to fall out of the sky
atribuirse a un fallo humano	to be attributed to human error

10.1.4 El transporte marítimo y fluvial

Sea and river transport

se tarda más	it takes longer
el ferry	(car) ferry
el muelle	quay
la hidroala	hydrofoil
el aerodeslizador	hovercraft
el petrolero	oil tanker
el transatlántico	liner
el buque de carga	freighter
el buque salvavidas	lifeboat
los canales del interior	inland waterways
el Canal de la Mancha	English Channel
el Golfo de Vizcaya	Bay of Biscay
el (Mar) Mediterráneo	Mediterranean (Sea)
el Estrecho de Gibraltar	Strait of Gibraltar
la travesía	crossing

marearse	to get seasick
naufragar	to be shipwrecked
ahogarse	to be drowned
hundirse	to sink
el rescate marítimo	sea rescue
el puesto de guardacostas	coastguard station

10.1.5 El transporte particular   *Private transport*

el permiso de conducir	driving licence
el código de circulación	Highway Code
el aparcamiento para turismos	parking for private cars
el aparcamiento subterráneo	underground car park
el parquímetro	parking meter
la multa de aparcamiento	parking ticket / fine
acelerar la marcha	to step on the accelerator, put one's foot down
adelantar	to overtake
la velocidad máxima	maximum speed
¡a más de 50 semáforo en rojo!	if you do more than 50kph the light will turn red! (traffic calming device common in Spain)
la zona de velocidad controlada por radar	speed-trap area
los detectores automáticos de velocidad	speed cameras / clocks
ponerle una multa a alguien en el acto	to fine sb on the spot
las cámaras en carretera	speed cameras
te quitan tres puntos de tu permiso de conducir	you collect three points on your driving licence
atropellar	to knock over, run over
tener un encontronazo	to have a collision
estrellarse contra	to crash into
chocar de frente	to crash head-on
patinar	to skid
el lesionado / la lesionada	casualty
tener una avería	to break down
estar averiado	to be broken down
hacer autostop / ir en autostop	to hitch-hike
el / la autostopista	hitch-hiker
compartir el coche	to 'car-share'
ofrecer llevarle a alguien	to offer someone a lift
prescindir del coche	to do without the car
dejar el coche en el garaje	to leave the car in the garage
un coche de alto consumo de gasolina	'gas guzzler'
incrementar el impuesto sobre el combustible	to increase the duty on fuel
el coche de gasoil	diesel car

el coche eléctrico / híbrido	electric / hybrid car
volver a descubrir la bicicleta	to rediscover the bicycle
el lobby ciclista	the cycling lobby
el alquiler gratuito de bicis	free bike hire

You will find further vocabulary on town traffic in Chapter 8.

10.2 El turismo y las vacaciones
Tourism and holidays

10.2.1 La industria turística
The tourist industry

el tour operador	tour operator
el paquete	package
el viaje con todo incluido	package tour
las zonas costeras	the coastal areas
los excursionistas	day-trippers
la localización geográfica	geographical situation
las playas están a rebosar	the beaches are overflowing
España está a tope de turistas	Spain is bursting with tourists
las previsiones para este año	the forecast for this year
se espera recibir a cuarenta millones de visitantes	forty million visitors are expected
estar a dos horas de vuelo de Londres	to be two hours' flight from London
llegar en el ferry desde Plymouth	to arrive on the Plymouth ferry
España es un país turísticamente muy organizado	Spain is a well-organised tourist destination
la relación precio-calidad	the price-quality ratio
el turismo de masas	mass tourism
el turismo de calidad	quality tourism
el turismo alternativo	alternative tourism
desarrollar el interior	to develop inland areas
dirigirse tierra adentro	to head inland
una ciudad monumental	a historic town
la zona monumental	the historic area
el casco antiguo	the old part (of town)
para el turista perspicaz	for the discerning tourist
un centro turístico de primera categoría	a first-class tourist centre
la industria hotelera	hotel industry
la estacionalidad	seasonal variation (of demand)
la temporada alta / baja	the high / low season
la infrautilización de la capacidad hotelera	the under-use of hotel accommodation / capacity
no se puede encontrar ni hotel ni apartamento	you can't find a hotel or an apartment
el coste del alojamiento	cost of accommodation
la doble reserva	double booking

el libro de reclamaciones	complaints book
formular una reclamación	to lodge / make a complaint
una habitación con vistas al mar	a room with a sea view
la habitación da a un solar	the room looks on to a building site
el gamberrismo	loutishness, yobbishness
las invasiones de gamberros extranjeros	invasion of foreign yobs

10.2.2 Las vacaciones — *Holidays*

olvidar la rutina diaria	to forget the daily routine
descansar del ajetreo cotidiano	to have a break from the daily grind
el crucero	cruise
para todos los gustos	for all tastes
disfrutar de unas buenas vacaciones	to enjoy a good holiday
a un precio al alcance de cualquiera	at a reasonable price
costearse unas vacaciones	to afford a holiday
no supone un gran desembolso	it doesn't involve a large outlay
desembolsar importantes sumas de dinero	to spend considerable sums of money
gastarse un dineral	to spend a small fortune
tomar el sol en la playa	to sunbathe on the beach
broncearse	to get a suntan
estar a sus anchas	to be at one's ease
escoger un sitio marchoso	to choose a trendy place
la movida nocturna	the night life
salir de marcha	to go out 'on the tiles'
ser noctámbulo	to be a night bird
pasarlo bomba (*coll*)	to have a whale of a time
buscarse unos días de paz y tranquilidad	to seek a few days' peace and quiet
un sitio alejado del ruido de las ciudades	a place far from the noise of the city
nada más relajante que ...	nothing more relaxing than ...
el ecoturismo	ecotourism
las vacaciones de aventura	adventure holidays
viajar con mochila	to backpack
el mochilero / la mochilera	backpacker
el parque temático	theme park

For further possible holiday activities see Chapter 7.

```
www.dgt.es
www.fomento.es
www.iberia.com
www.feve.es
www.renfe.es
```

Los medios

11.1 La televisión y la radio *Television and radio*

11.1.1 El sistema y los aparatos *The system and equipment*

la televisión	television (the medium)
el televisor	television (the set)
la tele	TV, telly
poner / quitar la tele	to turn the telly on / off
la televisión / radio digital	digital television / radio
el receptor	receiver
el transistor	transistor
el / la oyente	listener
el / la televidente ⎫	
el telespectador / la telespectadora ⎭	viewer (of television)
el programa	programme
la programación	programme times
el canal ⎫	
la cadena ⎭	channel
una gama amplia de canales	a wide range of channels
el espacio	(programme) slot
el monopolio público	public monopoly
el monopolio oficial televisivo	the official television monopoly
la empresa privada	private company
la pantalla chica	the small screen
la 'caja tonta'	'goggle box'
el mando a distancia	remote control
la televisión por cable	cable television
la televisión por satélite	satellite television
la (antena) parabólica	satellite dish
la emisora	broadcasting station, transmitter

11.1.2 El contenido

Programme content

una gama de programas	a range of programmes
la actualidad	current affairs
el telediario	TV news programme
las noticias	news (i.e. contents)
los anuncios	advertisements
la telenovela	soap opera
el dibujo animado	cartoon
el concurso	competition
el / la concursante	competitor
repetir por enésima vez	to repeat for the umpteenth time
el influjo sobre los valores morales	the influence on moral values
una gran ayuda educativa	a great educational aid
ejercer control sobre la selección de los programas	to exercise control over the choice of programmes
adaptar su propio horario al de la tele	to adapt one's own timetable to the TV
proporcionar cultura	to propagate culture
la violencia televisiva	television violence
dosificar el tiempo ante el televisor	to measure / ration time spent in front of the TV
avivar la imaginación	to sharpen the imagination
producir un efecto hipnótico	to have a hypnotic effect
una fuerza social destructora	a destructive social force
producir la pérdida de capacidad creativa	to bring about a loss of creativity
coartar la agilidad mental	to stultify mental agility
perjudicar el desarrollo del niño	to prejudice a child's development
el vídeo	video (all senses)
el DVD (dé-uve-dé)	DVD
la película de vídeo	videofilm
grabar en vídeo / DVD	to record on video / DVD
el videocasete	video cassette
la videograbadora	video recorder
el videofilm / DVD de terror	video / DVD nasty
la pornografía	pornography
la porno	porn
el vídeo porno	porn video
pornográfico/a	pornographic

11.2 La prensa   *The press*

el periódico	newspaper
el diario	daily paper
la revista semanal / mensual	weekly / monthly magazine
la revista deportiva / futbolística	sports / football magazine
la revista / prensa del corazón	glossy, romantic magazine / press (e.g. *¡Hola!*)
el 'tabloide'	tabloid
la circulación	circulation
el / la periodista	journalist
el reportero / la reportera	reporter
el redactor / la redactora	editor
redactar un periódico	to edit a newspaper
el artículo de fondo	editorial article
dar una rueda de prensa	to give a press conference
defender la libertad de la prensa	to defend the freedom of the press
la censura de la época franquista	the censorship of the Franco years
luchar contra el censor	to fight against the censor
aparecer en las columnas del periódico	to appear in the newspaper columns
los titulares proclaman ...	the headlines proclaim ...
tener prejuicios contra	to be biased against
ser partidario/a de	to be biased in favour of
tener propensión a	to be biased towards
un juicio parcial	biased judgement
apoyar una opinión política	to support a political opinion
la prensa sensacionalista	gutter press
la consultora sentimental	agony aunt
el triunfo	triumph, 'scoop'
invadir la intimidad de alguien	to invade somebody's privacy
se meten en todos sitios con sus cámaras	they get in everywhere with their cameras
demandar a alguien por difamación	to sue somebody for libel

la industria publicitaria	advertising industry
la agencia publicitaria	advertising agency
la cartelera	hoarding
ol cartel (publicitario)	(advertising) poster
el anuncio	advertisement
los pequeños anuncios	small ads
promocionar	to promote
el mensaje	message
la consignación de publicidad	advertising budget
el eslogan publicitario	advertising slogan
llamativo/a	appealing, eye-catching
la propaganda de buzón	junk mail
el mercado objetivo	target market
hacer impacto (en)	to make an impact (on)
manipular	to manipulate
persuadir (a)	to persuade (to)
tentar (a)	to tempt (to)
llamar a nuestros instintos más bajos	to appeal to our baser instincts
el lavado de cerebro	brainwashing
obrar en el subconsciente de alguien	to work on sb's subconscious
subconscientemente	subconsciously
una persona de voluntad débil	a weak-willed person
el consumidor / la consumidora	consumer
la sociedad consumista	consumer society
el poder adquisitivo	purchasing power
codiciar	to covet
acumular deudas con la tarjeta de crédito	to build up credit-card debts
la interrupción constante de los programas	constant interruption of programmes
la actitud sexista de los anunciantes	the sexist attitude of the advertisers
dirigirse al consumidor joven	to target the young consumer

---

www.rtve.es
www.telemadrid.es

Pages iv–v also contain a list of press websites.

12.1 La infraestructura sanitaria

	Health infrastructure
el médico / la médica	doctor, GP
el enfermero / la enfermera	nurse
el / la dentista	dentist
la salud	health (personal)
la sanidad	health (public)
INSALUD (el Instituto Nacional de la Salud)	Spanish NHS (National Health Service)
el Ministerio de Sanidad	Ministry of Health
el ambulatorio / el centro de salud	(local) health centre
la medicina	medicine (subject)
la atención médica	medical care
el / la especialista	specialist
el cirujano / la cirujana	surgeon
la cirugía	surgery (operation)
la clínica	clinic
el consultorio	clinic, consulting room, surgery (in this sense)
quirúrgico/a	surgical

12.2 Las condiciones médicas y sus síntomas

Medical conditions and their symptoms

estar enfermo/a	to be ill
ser enfermo/a	to be an invalid (i.e. permanent)
caer enfermo/a (de) / enfermar (de)	to fall ill (with), go down (with)
el tratamiento	treatment
el microbio	microbe, 'bug'
el virus	virus
la epidemia	epidemic
la pandemia	pandemic
la alergia	allergy
alérgico/a	allergic
tener alergia a	to be allergic to
el síndrome de alergia total	total allergy syndrome
el agotamiento	exhaustion
el estrés / la tensión	stress
estar hecho/a polvo	to feel a wreck
no poder más	to be at the end of one's tether
desvelarse	to be unable to sleep, to lie awake

el cansancio físico y mental	physical and mental tiredness
echar mano a un medicamento	to reach for the medicine
contagiarse (de)	to become infected (with), to catch
evitar contagios	to avoid infection
el trastorno	upset, trouble
el período de incubación	incubation period
pasar desapercibido/a	to go unnoticed, undetected
padecer una dolencia	to suffer from an illness
el minusválido / la minusválida	disabled person
la minusvalía	disability
tener una lesión grave	to have a serious injury
las enfermedades invernales	coughs and colds, winter illnesses
la diabetes	diabetes
(ser) diabético/a	(to be) diabetic
la pulmonía	pneumonia
el SIDA (síndrome de inmunodeficiencia adquirida)	AIDS
el VIH (virus de la inmunodeficiencia humana)	HIV
ser seropositivo/a	to be HIV positive
el sistema Inmunológico	immune system
transmitir por los fluidos corporales	to transmit via body fluids
el cáncer del pulmón	lung cancer
el infarto	heart attack
las enfermedades cardíacas	heart disease
la viruola	smallpox
el paludismo	malaria
la amigdalitis	tonsillitis
la bronquitis crónica	chronic bronchitis*
la tuberculosis	tuberculosis*

* Most diseases which end in '-is' in English are identical in Spanish except for adaptation to the Spanish spelling system (e.g. bronquitis). They are always feminine.

la gripe aviar	bird flu
la gripe A	swine flu
la gripe estacional	seasonal flu
envejecer	to age
la salud mental	mental health
la enfermedad mental	mental illness
la depresión	depression
deprimirse	to become depressed
estar acomplejado/a	to have a complex
recibir tratamiento psiquiátrico	to undergo psychiatric treatment
el / la psiquiatra	psychiatrist
el colapso nervioso	nervous breakdown
padecer de los nervios	to suffer from one's nerves
los nervios se me disparan	my nerves are at breaking point
tener los nervios destrozados	to be a nervous wreck

suicidarse	to commit suicide
el suicidio	suicide (act)
el / la suicida	suicide (person)
la tentativa de suicidio	suicide attempt
la regla	(menstrual) period

12.3 El tratamiento y los remedios

Treatment and remedies

¡que te mejores pronto!	get well soon!
la farmacia	pharmacy, chemist shop
el farmacéutico / la farmacéutica	pharmacist, chemist
el medicamento	medicine (which you take)
la receta	prescription
el diagnóstico	diagnosis
curar	to cure, treat
curarse	to recover, get better, be healed
reponerse	to recover
se vende sólo con receta	obtainable only on prescription
recetar una droga	to prescribe a drug
las contraindicaciones	contraindications
los efectos secundarios	side-effects
el somnífero	sleeping tablet
el tranquilizante	tranquilliser
el analgésico	analgesic, painkiller
hospitalizar	to hospitalise, put into hospital
pasar un rato en el hospital	to spend a while in hospital
la casa / sala de maternidad	maternity hospital / ward
la terapia	therapy
seguir un curso de fisioterapia	to follow a course of physiotherapy
el / la fisioterapeuta	physiotherapist
operarse	to have an operation
me (le) operaron el pie	I (s/he) had a foot operation
el equipo médico de urgencia	emergency medical team
un descongestivo nasal	a nasal decongestant
sonarse las narices	to blow one's nose
limpiarse los mocos	to wipe one's nose
las más avanzadas técnicas en cirugía	the most advanced surgical techniques
el tratamiento curativo	curative treatment
la anestesia general / local	general / local anaesthetic
anestesiar	to anaesthetise, give an anaesthetic to
el trasplante de hígado	liver transplant
el / la donante de órganos / riñón	organ / kidney donor
rechazar el órgano trasplantado	to reject the transplant
trasplantar	to transplant

responder al tratamiento	to respond to treatment
la hormona	hormone
la píldora	pill
el comprimido	tablet
la transfusión de sangre	blood transfusion

12.4 La medicina preventiva *Preventive medicine*

la educación sanitaria	health education
más vale prevenir que curar	prevention is better than cure
promocionar la salud	to promote health
estar en buena forma / condición	to be in good physical shape
mantenerse en forma física	to keep fit
la higiene	hygiene
llevar un modo de vida sano	to lead a healthy life
la necesidad del ejercicio regular	the need for regular exercise
la función vital	vital function
preocuparse por la salud	to worry about one's health
pasar una revisión médica	to have a medical examination
el chequeo	check-up
la exploración (médica)	(medical) investigation, check-up
tomarse la tensión arterial	to take one's (own) blood pressure
detectar a tiempo	to detect in time
atajar la aparición de enfermedades	to forestall the onset of disease
un diagnóstico precoz de determinadas dolencias	early diagnosis of certain illnesses
comprobarse el nivel del colesterol	to check one's cholesterol level
la vacuna	vaccine
vacunarse contra	to be vaccinated against
diagnosticar	to diagnose
el autodiagnóstico	self-diagnosis
autodiagnosticarse	to make a self-diagnosis
poner de manifiesto	to bring to light
tener propensión especial a un determinado mal	to be particularly susceptible to a specific complaint
los signos clínicos	the clinical signs
darse un respiro	to give oneself a break
el ritmo biológico	biological rhythm
la longevidad	life expectancy
la natalidad	birth rate
la mortalidad	death rate

12.5 El régimen

Diet

el régimen ⎱ la dieta ⎰	diet
una dieta sana	a healthy diet
una epidemia de obesidad	an obesity epidemic
ser obeso/a	to be obese
el peso	weight
pesar demasiado	to be overweight
el índice de masa corporal	body mass index
comer compulsivamente	to be a compulsive eater
engordar	to put on weight
engordar ocho kilos	to put on eight kilos
tener doce kilos de más	to be twelve kilos overweight
esos kilos de más	that extra weight
los 'michelines'	'spare tyre'
la materia grasa	fatty substances, fat
los ingredientes calóricos	high-calorie ingredients
una nutrición equilibrada	a balanced intake / diet
el aporte justo de calorías	the right number of calories
quemar las materias grasas	to burn off fat
tener una obsesión por adelgazar	to have a slimming obsession
adelgazar cinco kilos	to lose five kilos
quitarse dos kilos	to take off two kilos
cuidarse la línea	to watch one's figure
sentir hambre	to feel hungry
la anorexia nerviosa	anorexia nervosa
el pan integral	wholemeal bread
la fibra	fibre
la energía	energy
un alimento muy energético	a high-energy food

12.6 El tabaco y el alcohol

Tobacco and alcohol

fumar en pipa	to smoke a pipe (as opposed to cigarettes)
fumarse una pipa	to smoke a pipe (a pipeful)
dejar de fumar	to give up smoking
inhalar	to inhale
los cigarrillos con menos nicotina y alquitrán	cigarettes with reduced nicotine and tar
el tabaquismo	tobacco habit, addiction
la ley antitabaco	anti-smoking law
en caso de que te resulte imposible abandonar el cigarrillo	in the event of your being unable to give up cigarettes
perjudicar seriamente la salud	to seriously affect one's health
destrozarse los pulmones	to wreck one's lungs
el excesivo consumo de alcohol	excessive alcohol consumption

beber alcohol en ayunas	to drink alcohol on an empty stomach
afecta a todo el organismo	it affects the whole system
los trastornos cardiocirculatorios	cardiovascular problems
la intoxicación aguda	acute intoxication
la borrachera	drunken state, binge
la capacidad de reflejos	reflex capacity
el nivel de alcohol en la sangre	blood-alcohol level
ingerir en pequeñas dosis	to take in small doses
la resaca	hangover
someter a la prueba del alcoholímetro	to breathalyse

12.7 La droga — *Drugs*

el estupefaciente	narcotic
el depresor	depressant
los barbitúricos	barbiturates
la droga dura / blanda	hard / soft drug
el drogadicto / la drogadicta } el toxicómano / la toxicómana	drug addict
la drogadicción	drug addiction
la toxicomanía galopante	accelerating drug addiction
la drogodependencia	drug dependency
el / la drogodependiente	person dependent on drugs
la cocaína	cocaine
la 'coca'	coke, cocaine (not 'Coca-Cola'!)
el cocainómano / la cocainómana	cocaine addict
la heroína	heroin
el heroinómano / la heroinómana	heroin addict
el narcotráfico	drugs traffic
el / la narcotraficante	drug trafficker
el / la camello (*coll*)	drug pusher
la marijuana	marijuana, cannabis
el chocolate	'dope', cannabis
el porro	joint, cannabis cigarette
penalizar el consumo de drogas en lugares públicos	to make the consumption of drugs in public places illegal
la legalización (parcial) de las drogas	the (partial) legalisation of drugs
legalizar	to legalise
el / la yonqui	junkie
esnifar	to sniff
el esnifamiento de disolvente	solvent abuse, glue-sniffing
la jeringuilla	syringe
inyectarse	to inject (oneself)
pincharse (*coll*)	to 'shoot up'
engancharse	to get hooked
estar enganchado/a } estar colgado/a	to be hooked
costearse un vicio	to afford a vice

drogarse	to take drugs
doparse	to take dope
probar una droga	to try (out) a drug
estar totalmente en contra de la droga	to be totally against drugs
un programa de reinserción social	a programme of social rehabilitation
un programa de desintoxicación	a detoxification programme
el síndrome de abstinencia	withdrawal symptoms
tener el mono	to go 'cold turkey'
estar rabiando por un pinchazo	to be craving for a fix
la dosis fatal	fatal dose

www.dietas.com
www.cruzroja.es
www.msc.es
www.madrid.org/sanidad

13.1 Las artes visuales — *Visual arts*

el dibujo	drawing
dibujar	to draw
la exposición	exhibition
la colección	collection
representar	to represent
pintar	to paint
la pintura	painting
el pintor / la pintora	painter
pintoresco	picturesque
el cuadro	picture
el retrato	portrait
retratar	to portray, paint a portrait of
el diseño	design
diseñar	to design
la escultura	sculpture
esculpir	to sculpt
el escultor / la escultora	sculptor
el arte abstracto	abstract art
el símbolo	symbol
simbolizar	to symbolise
el lienzo	canvas
la acuarela	watercolour
la pintura al óleo	oil painting
pintar al óleo	to paint in oils
el bodegón	still life
representar	to depict
el pincel	paintbrush
la pincelada	brush stroke
el contraste de la luz y sombra	contrast of light and shadow
especializarse en la representación de la forma humana	to specialise in the depiction of the human form
no pertenece a ninguna escuela reconocida	s/he doesn't belong to any recognised school
tiene su estilo individual	s/he has his / her own individual style
el museo de bellas artes	fine arts museum
la galería	gallery
de la escuela impresionista	of the Impressionist school
la venta	sale
vender por una cifra elevada	to sell for a high price
el lote	lot

la subasta	auction
la puja	bid
pujar	to bid
la obra maestra	masterwork, masterpiece
el aficionado / la aficionada	fan, enthusiast

13.2 El cine y el teatro — *Cinema and theatre*

13.2.1 En general — *In general*

la taquilla	box office
el actor / la actriz	actor / actress
las butacas	stalls
la localidad	seat
el rol / el papel	role
el / la protagonista	main role, protagonist
protagonizar	to play the main part / protagonist
una película / obra protagonizada por X	a film / play with X in the leading role
desempeñar un papel	to play a part / role
despertó mucho interés con su primera película / primer papel	s/he aroused a great deal of interest with his / her first film / role
a lo largo de su carrera	throughout his / her career
el estreno	first showing / performance
estrenar una película / una obra	to put on a film / play for the first time
gozar del cine / del teatro	to enjoy the cinema / theatre
explorar nuevos horizontes	to explore new horizons
la subvención gubernamental	government subsidy
patrocinar las bellas artes	to sponsor the fine arts
bajo el patrocinio de	under the sponsorship of
contar con el apoyo del Ministerio de Cultura	to rely on the support of the Ministry of Culture

13.2.2 El cine — *Cinema*

el film(e) (*pl* films *or* filmes) la película	film
la pantalla	screen
la estrella de cine	film star
rodar una película	to shoot a film
el largometraje	full-length film, feature film
el cortometraje	'short' (film)
el documental	documentary
el guión	script
el / la guionista	scriptwriter
el director / la directora	director
el / la cineasta	film maker

doblar en castellano	to dub into Spanish
la banda sonora	sound track
los subtítulos	subtitles
la película está subtitulada en catalán	the film is subtitled in Catalan
para todos los públicos	suitable for all ages
no recomendada a menores de trece años	not suitable for under-13s
la sesión continua	continuous performance
la película en conjunto	the film as a whole
la movida madrileña	the Madrid 'scene'

13.2.3 El teatro

Theatre

la obra (de teatro)	play
poner una obra en escena	to produce a play
la puesta en escena	production
interpretar una obra	to perform / interpret a play
la interpretación	performance, interpretation
actuar	to act
la actuación	the acting
la comedia	comedy
la tragedia	tragedy
el drama	drama
el espectáculo teatral	(theatre) show
la escena el escenario	stage
el montaje	design, décor
la obra está ambientada en Sevilla	the play is set in Seville
la trama es muy enrevesada	the plot is very involved
el desenlace	outcome, dénouement
al caer el telón	when the curtain falls / fell
aplaudir	to applaud
los aplausos	applause
silbar	to hiss, boo
ante el público	in front of the audience
el miedo a salir a la escena	stage fright
el maquillaje	make-up
maquillarse	to put one's make-up on
el teatro callejero	street theatre
los títeres	puppets
la temporada	season (theatre, etc.)
subvencionar el teatro	to subsidise the theatre

13.3 La literatura / *Literature*

la lectura	reading
el lector / la lectora	reader
el autor / la autora	author
el escritor / la escritora	writer
el editor / la editora	editor
la biblioteca	library
el bibliotecario / la bibliotecaria	librarian
la librería	bookshop
el librero / la librera	bookseller
la novela	novel
el libro de bolsillo	paperback
el género	genre
el cuento	short story, tale
el / la cuentista	short story writer
la (auto)biografía	(auto)biography
(auto)biográfico/a	(auto)biographical
la novela policíaca	detective novel
la poesía	poetry, poem
la obra poética	poetic work
es un(a) apasionado/a de la ciencia-ficción	s/he is a science-fiction addict
el estilo	style
la narración	narrative
la historia se localiza en Madrid	the story is set in Madrid
el desenlace es una verdadera sorpresa	the outcome is a real surprise
saber contar una historia	to know how to tell a story, be a good storyteller
el cuento alcanza su desenlace	the story unfolds
el escritor / la escritora de vanguardia	avant-garde writer
la (casa) editorial	publishing house
los derechos de autor	royalties
ser un ratón de biblioteca	to be a bookworm
disfrutar de una buena lectura	to enjoy a good read
en toda su obra	in the whole of his / her work
el premio Nobel de literatura	the Nobel Prize for literature
la tirada	edition, print run
la reproducción ilegal	illegal copying

13.4 La música   *Music*

la música	music
el / la músico	musician (male or female)
la sala de conciertos	concert hall
el auditorio	concert hall, auditorium
la orquesta de cámara	chamber orchestra
la orquesta filarmónica	philharmonic orchestra
el coro	choir
el compositor / la compositora	composer
componer	to compose
la partitura	score (musical)
la quinta sinfonía de Beethoven	Beethoven's fifth symphony
una gran obra sinfónica	a great symphonic work
el concierto en si bemol menor de Chaikovski	Tchaikovsky's B flat minor concerto
la ópera	opera
el aria (f) operática	operatic aria
la zarzuela	Spanish light opera
el / la cantante	singer
el cantaor / la cantaora	flamenco singer (only)
el cantautor / la cantautora	singer-songwriter
cantar	to sing
el / la instrumentalista	instrumentalist
el / la solista	soloist
ser clarinetista	to be a clarinettist
tocar la flauta	to play the flute
el director / la directora	conductor
la orquesta fue dirigida por ...	the orchestra was conducted by ...
bajo la batuta de ...	under the baton of ...
el primer violín	leader, first violin
ser muy aficionado/a a Rodrigo	to be very fond of Rodrigo
tocar música en la calle	to busk
el / la músico ambulante	busker
la música pop	pop music
el conjunto de pop	pop group
el concierto	gig (of pop music)
el / la rockero/a	rock singer, rock fan
el sencillo	single (disc)
el elepé	LP (long-play record)
el CD, disco compacto	CD, compact disc
descargar	to download

NB: *Many types of popular music are known by their English names: jazz, soul, rock, blues, reggae, punk, etc, and have no Spanish equivalent. There is more vocabulary concerning pop music in Section 4.4.*

13.5 La crítica

Criticism

el crítico / la crítica de teatro / cine / música	theatre / film / music critic
se publicó en	it was published in
se estrenó en	it was first shown / performed in
analizar	to analyse
citar	to quote
la citación	quotation
es un(a) película / obra / papel / personaje / libro ...	it is a ... film / play / role / character / book
ameno/a	pleasant
chocarrero/a	scurrilous
deprimente	depressing
divertido	funny
exigente	demanding
esotérico/a	esoteric / highbrow
enrevesado/a	involved
humorístico/a	humorous
ligero/a	light
pesado/a	tedious
salado/a	witty
satírico/a	satirical
sobresaliente	outstanding

Remember to make the adjective agree correctly!

se criticó de lento/a y pesado/a	it was criticised for being slow and tedious
¡dos horas de carcajadas!	two hours of laughter!
logra que el público se ría del principio al fin	s/he manages to get the audience laughing from beginning to end
mantener la tensión a lo largo de toda la representación	to keep up the tension throughout the performance
es todo un espectáculo	it's quite a show
la brillante interpretación de los actores	the brilliant performance by the actors
demuestra su calidad de primera	s/he demonstrates his/her first-rate skill
el secreto del gran actor	the secret of the great actor
fue un fracaso total	it was an utter flop
fracasar	to fail, flop
al leer / ver esta escena	when I read / saw this scene
mi primera reacción fue (+ *n* or *inf*)	my first reaction was (+ *n* or *to* ...)
me encantó la yuxtaposición de ... y ...	I loved the juxtaposition of ... and ...
el uso de la poesía / del baile	the use of poetry / dance
de esto se puede inferir que ...	from this we can infer that ...
está escrito en prosa	it is written in prose
tiene un estilo muy lírico	s/he has a very lyrical style

You will find further words and phrases which could be used to describe film or literary characters in Chapter 2, and further leisure activities in Chapter 7.

www.mcu.es
www.terra.es/cine *or* /teatro *or* /musica

El medio ambiente

14.1 El ecosistema

The ecosystem

14.1.1 Problemas y soluciones en general

Problems and solutions in general

el entorno natural	natural surroundings / environment
la amenaza a la naturaleza	the threat to wildlife
amenazar / trastornar el equilibrio ecológico	to threaten / upset the ecological balance
modificar el ecosistema	to change the ecosystem
el deterioro ambiental	environmental damage
la huella de carbono	carbon footprint
la huella ecológica	ecological footprint
causar daños irreversibles	to cause irreversible damage
la supervivencia del hombre	man's survival
un planeta moribundo	a dying planet
las oportunidades de reducir las emisiones	opportunities to reduce emissions
reducir los daños causados a ...	to reduce the damage caused to ...
desatender las advertencias de los científicos	to disregard the scientists' warnings
el empeoramiento de la calidad de la vida	deterioration in the quality of life

14.1.2 Motivos específicos de preocupación

Specific areas of concern

el cambio climático	climate change
el recalentamiento del planeta ⎫ el calentamiento del globo ⎭	global warming
el efecto invernadero	greenhouse effect
los gases invernadero	greenhouse gases
la destrucción de la capa de ozono	destruction of the ozone layer
el agujero de ozono	hole in the ozone layer
el clorofluorocarbono	chlorofluorocarbon, CFC
los hidrocarburos	hydrocarbons
el spray	spray, aerosol
el aerosol	aerosol
echar / vomitar humos	to belch out smoke
los gases contaminantes	polluting gases
x toneladas de dióxido de carbono	x tons of carbon dioxide
las lluvias ácidas	acid rain

la destrucción de las selvas tropicales	destruction of the rain forests
la deforestación	deforestation
la desertización	desertification
las radiaciones ultravioletas	ultraviolet radiation
el derretimiento de la capa de hielo polar	melting of the polar ice sheet
derretirse	to melt (*intrans*)
el aumento del nivel del mar	rise in sea level
con sólo dos grados de más	with only two degrees (C) more
con toda urgencia	with the utmost urgency
el movimiento ecologista mundial	world ecology movement
nos quedan veinte años para evitar una catástrofe climática	we have 20 years left to avert a climatic disaster
la velocidad actual del recalentamiento del planeta es insostenible	the present rate of global warming is unsustainable
la temperatura a la que resultará imposible frenar los cambios	the temperature at which it will be impossible to stop changes
la utilización pacífica de la energía nuclear	peaceful use of nuclear energy
reanudar la construcción de centrales nucleares	to resume the building of nuclear power stations
el viento y el aire no conocen fronteras	the wind and the air know no frontiers
despertar a la opinión pública	to awaken public opinion
luchar por la supervivencia de las especies	to fight for the survival of species

14.2 La energía

Energy

14.2.1 Los recursos naturales

Natural resources

los recursos energéticos	energy resources
el consumo de recursos naturales	the consumption of natural resources
el consumo de energía	energy consumption
el ahorro de energía	the saving of energy
conservar los escasos recursos del planeta	to conserve the planet's scarce resources
los recursos se agotan	resources are being exhausted
la pérdida de recursos valiosos	the loss of valuable resources
el despilfarro	wastefulness, squandering
despilfarrar	to squander
conservar la energía	to conserve energy
el aislamiento térmico	heat insulation
encender / apagar la calefacción	to switch the heating on / off
dejar encendidas las luces	to leave the lights on

los combustibles fósiles	fossil fuels
el petróleo	crude oil
consumir un x% de todos los recursos del mundo	to consume x% of all the world's resources
el uso racional de la energía disponible	the rational use of available energy
satisfacer las necesidades de los países industrializados	to meet the needs of the industrialised countries
cuando el petróleo llegue a x dólares el barril	when oil reaches x dollars a barrel
los países del Cercano Oriente	Middle Eastern countries
la crisis de petróleo	oil crisis
sacar de la tierra	to take out of the ground
la central térmica convencional	conventional power station
minar	to mine
los adelantos técnicos	technical advances
la mayor fuente de energía utilizable	the greatest source of usable energy
tomar medidas	to take measures
las reservas sin explotar	unexploited reserves
ejercer una enorme presión sobre	to exert an enormous pressure on
una política de conservación	a conservation policy
los recursos renovables	renewable resources
la energía eólica	wind energy
el aerogenerador	wind turbine
el parque eólico	wind farm
aprovechar la energía de las olas	to harness the energy of the waves
la central hidroeléctrica	hydroelectric power station
la hidroelectricidad	hydroelectricity
el apagón	blackout, power failure

14.2.2 La energía nuclear

Nuclear energy

radioactivo/a	radioactive
una fuga de radioactividad	a radioactive leak
el siniestro nuclear	nuclear disaster
el reactor	reactor
la explosión	explosion
explotar	to explode
la energía limpia	clean energy
una nueva generación de centrales (f) nucleares	a new generation of nuclear power stations
montar una campaña antinuclear	to mount an anti-nuclear campaign
el contador Geiger registra ...	the Geiger counter registers ...
alcanzar la fusión	to reach meltdown
un blanco para terroristas	a terrorist target
como consecuencia de Chernóbil	in the aftermath of Chernobyl

14.3 La contaminación   *Pollution*

14.3.1 La tierra, el mar y el aire   *Land, sea and air*

la basura	rubbish
el vertedero	rubbish tip
verter al mar	to tip into the sea
producir efectos tóxicos	to have toxic effects
contaminar	to pollute, contaminate
los contaminantes atmosféricos	atmospheric pollutants
la contaminación atmosférica transfronteriza	cross-frontier atmospheric pollution
la descontaminación	decontamination
descontaminar	to decontaminate
la central nuclear	nuclear power station
los residuos radioactivos	radioactive waste
los efectos nocivos	harmful effects
el reactor nuclear	nuclear reactor
la nocividad de las emisiones	the harmful nature of emissions
sobrepasar la capacidad de absorción de la naturaleza	to go beyond nature's ability to absorb
estar enterado/a de la amenaza	to be aware of the threat
los países nuclearizados	countries with nuclear capacity
satisfacer las necesidades de la sociedad consumista	to meet the needs of the consumer society
reutilizar las bolsas de plástico	to reuse plastic bags
tirar las basuras al contenedor que les corresponde	to put rubbish into the correct bin
los envases de cartón	cardboard packaging
envenenar	to poison
venenoso/a	poisonous
la mancha de petróleo	oil slick
limpiar los vertidos de petróleo	to clean up oil spills
aves marinas con su plumaje empapado de petróleo	seabirds with their feathers saturated with oil
el reciclaje de los desperdicios / la basura	recycling of waste
reciclar	to recycle

14.3.2 La contaminación sonora   *Noise pollution*

el nivel sonoro máximo	maximum noise level
los trastornos auditivos	hearing disorders
no debería sobrepasar los 70 decibelios	it shouldn't go above 70 decibels
el desmadre sonoro	the appalling noise level, infernal racket
la insonorización	soundproofing
insonorizar una casa	to soundproof a house
el aislamiento acústico / térmico	sound / heat insulation

---

www.mma.es
www.conama.cl
www.greenpeace.org/espana *or other relevant country after the slash*
www.wwf.es

15 La ciencia y la tecnología

15.1 La informática

Information technology

15.1.1 El ordenador

The computer

la revolución informática	information technology revolution
abrir / cerrar una ventana	to open / close a window
acceder al sistema	to log on
el acceso a la información	access to information
la clave de acceso ⎱	
la contraseña ⎰	password
almacenar	to store
el almacenamiento de datos	data storage
de alto rendimiento	(of) high-performance
apagar	to switch off
el archivo	file
archivar	to save
arrastrar	to drag
la barra espaciadora	space bar
bloquearse	to crash
borrar	to delete
el chip	chip
comprobar la ortografía	to spellcheck
la conexión de redes	networking
la conexión inalámbrica	wireless connection
la copia de seguridad	back-up copy
el cursor	cursor
mover el cursor	to move the cursor
los datos	data
la base / el banco de datos	database / bank
la ley de protección de datos	data protection law
el disco compacto / CD	compact disc / CD
el disco duro	hard disk
la unidad de disco	disk drive
el disquete	floppy disk
el disquete de reserva	back-up disk
editar	to edit
eliminar	to delete
el escáner	scanner
la fuente	font
el hardware	hardware
la imagen (*pl* imágenes)	picture
la impresora	printer

encender la impresora	to switch the printer on
la impresora de inyección de tinta a color	ink-jet colour printer
el sistema de impresión inyección de burbujas	bubble jet printing system
la impresora láser	laser printer
imprimir	to print, print out
informatizar	to computerise
el joystick	joystick
el listado	printout
el menú	menu
hacer aparecer el menú	to call up the menu
el monitor	monitor
el ordenador	computer
el ordenador portátil	laptop computer
la pantalla	screen, VDU
pegar	to paste
el / la pirata informático/a	hacker
el píxel	pixel
la potencia	power
procesar	to process
el procesador de textos	word processor
programar	to program
la programación	programming
el programador / la programadora	programmer
pulsar	to press (key), click (mouse)
pinchar	to click
pinchar / pulsar dos veces	to double click
al pulsar un botón	at the push of a button
el ratón	mouse
salir del sistema	to log off
el software	software
suprimir	to delete
el tabulador	tabulator
el teclado	keyboard
la tecla	key (of keyboard)
teclear	to type

15.1.2 Internet

The internet

acceder a la red	to access the web
la arroba	@
la banda ancha	broadband
el blog (*pl* blogs)	blog
buscar	to search
el buscador el motor de búsqueda }	search engine
la búsqueda	search

el correo electrónico	email (i.e. the system)
mandar por correo electrónico	to send by email, to email
el e-mail	email (i.e. the document sent or received)
el emilio (*coll*)	email
conectarse con	to connect / link up with
el costo de la conexión a Internet	the cost of internet connection
descargar	to download
la dirección	address
eliminar un virus	to get rid of a virus
el enlace	link
la hoja de cálculo	spreadsheet
Internet (*usually without definite article*)	the internet
el módem	modem
navegar	to surf (i.e. the web), browse
el navegador	browser
el / la navegante } el / la internauta }	(web) surfer
la página web	web page
piratear música	to pirate / illegally download music
la red	the web
el servidor	server
el spam	spam
la superautopista	superhighway
la web	the web / website

15.1.3 Los beneficios de la informática

Benefits of IT

los adelantos tecnológicos	technological advances
ahorrar tiempo y dinero	to save time and money
desarrollar	to develop
trabajar con más eficacia	to work more effectively
aprovechar los adelantos científicos	to benefit from scientific advances
asimilar las nuevas tecnologías	to assimilate the new technologies
el desarrollo científico	scientific development
la innovación técnica	technical innovation
nuevos recursos para los directivos	new resources for management
una sociedad evolucionada	a developed society
transformar la cultura humana	to transform / change human culture
transmitir e intercambiar información	to transmit and exchange information

15.2 Otros chismes tecnológicos

Other technological gadgetry

la alarma antirrobo	anti-theft alarm
la alarma antiincendios	fire alarm
la batidora	food mixer
la caja de control	control box
el cajero automático	automatic cash dispenser
la calculadora	calculator
la cerradura electrónica	electronic locking
los electrodomésticos	electrical appliances for the home
el detector de humo	smoke detector
activar	to set off
desactivar	to deactivate
el DVD (dé-uve-dé)	DVD
el enchufe	power point
enchufar	to plug in
desenchufar	to unplug
el equipo de hi-fi	hi-fi equipment
el facsímil(e) / fax	facsimile / fax
mandar por fax } faxear }	to fax
¿puede faxeármelo?	can you fax it to me?
la fotocopia	photocopy
la fotocopiadora	photocopier
fotocopiar	to photocopy
el horno microondas	microwave oven
el lavaplatos	dishwasher
la lavadora	washing machine
el lector de CDs	CD player
grabar	to record
el MP3 (eme-pé-tres)	MP3
el sistema de navegación por satélite	satellite navigation system
el robot de cocina	food processor
la secadora	tumble-drier
el secador de pelo	hairdrier
el sintonizador digital	digital tuner
sintonizar	to tune (in)
el sistema de seguridad	security system
el teléfono inalámbrico	cordless phone
el (teléfono) portátil } el móvil }	mobile (phone)
marcar un número	to dial a number

el mando a distancia	remote control, zapper
la televisión por satélite / cable	satellite / cable television
la antena parabólica	satellite dish
la televisión / radio digital	digital television / radio
el vídeo	video, video recorder
el videograbadora	video recorder

15.3 El personal, los procesos y las sustancias

People, processes and substances

el científico / la científica	scientist
el tecnólogo / la tecnóloga	technologist
la física	physics
el físico / la física	physicist
la química	chemistry
el químico / la química	chemist
la zoología	zoology
el zoólogo / la zoóloga	zoologist
investigar	to research
el investigador / la investigadora	researcher
promover las investigaciones científicas	to promote scientific research
seguir una línea de investigación	to follow a line of investigation
la sustancia	substance
el elemento	element
el compuesto	compound
el proceso	process
el laboratorio	laboratory
pasar por un circuito	to pass through a circuit
el oxígeno	oxygen
el hidrógeno	hydrogen
el nitrógeno	nitrogen
el monóxido / dióxido de carbono	carbon monoxide / dioxide
el mercurio	mercury
el plomo	lead
el complejo petroquímico	petrochemical complex

15.4 La exploración del espacio

Space exploration

el satélite meteorológico	meteorological satellite
la longitud de onda	wavelength
poner en órbita	to put into orbit
el transbordador espacial	space shuttle
la lanzadera espacial	space launch pad
lanzar	to launch
la nave (espacial)	(space) ship
la cápsula lunar	lunar capsule
el satélite de comunicaciones	communications satellite
la estación espacial	space station
acoplarse	to dock

www.mityc.es (*includes various links*)
www.terra.es/personal/lermon/esp/enciclo.htm (*good for computer vocabulary!*)

La religión

16.1 Las religiones — *Religions*

el cristianismo	Christianity
ser cristiano/a	to be a Christian
Dios	God
Jesús / Jesucristo	Jesus / Jesus Christ
el Padre, el Hijo y el Espíritu Santo	Father, Son and Holy Ghost
la Virgen María	the Virgin Mary
la (Santa) Biblia	the (Holy) Bible
el evangelio	the gospel
el catolicismo	Catholicism
la iglesia católica	the Catholic Church
el protestantismo	Protestantism
ser protestante	to be a Protestant
el Islam	Islam
musulmán / musulmana (*n* + *adj*)	Muslim
Alá	Allah
el profeta Mahoma	the prophet Mohammed
la mezquita	mosque
el Corán	Qur'an
el judaísmo	Judaism
el judío / la judía	Jew, Jewish
sionista (*n* + *adj*)	Zionist
el sinagoga	synagogue
el hinduismo	Hinduism
el budismo	Buddhism
Buda	Buddha
la deidad	deity
la diosa	goddess

16.2 Las jerarquías religiosas — *Religious hierarchies*

el Papa	the Pope
el arzobispo de Toledo	the Archbishop of Toledo
el obispo de Sevilla	the Bishop of Seville
el cura / el sacerdote	priest
el párroco	parish priest
la parroquia	parish, parish church
el santo / la santa	saint

el ayatolá	ayatollah
el imán	imam
el mullah	mullah
el rabí	rabbi

16.3 La doctrina religiosa — *Religious doctrine*

crucificar	to crucify
la crucifixión	crucifixion
el crucifijo	crucifix
la ortodoxia religiosa	religious orthodoxy
la virginidad	virginity
el nacimiento sin mancha	virgin birth
la resurrección	resurrection
el cielo	heaven
el paraíso	paradise
el ángel	angel
el infierno	hell
el milagro	miracle
el diablo	the devil
Satanás	Satan

16.4 La práctica de la religión — *Religious practice*

el oficio	service
el culto	worship
rezar	to pray
las oraciones	prayers
bautizar a un niño	to christen / baptise a child
casarse por la iglesia	to get married in church
ir a misa	to go to mass
la primera comunión	first communion
la confirmación	confirmation
ayunar	to fast
el ramadán	Ramadan
el sábado (Jewish); el domingo (Christian)	Sabbath
practicar / abrazar una religión	to practise / embrace a religion
predicar	to preach

16.5 Las creencias religiosas *Religious beliefs*

creer en Dios	to believe in God
ser creyente	to be a believer
profesar una fe	to profess a faith
ser católico/a practicante	to be a practising Catholic
tener / sentir una vocación religiosa	to have / feel a religious vocation
dar sentido a la vida	to give meaning to life
manifestarse de acuerdo con el Papa	to come out in agreement with the Pope
sentir un vacío	to feel a gap / an emptiness
rechazar	to reject
ser escéptico/a	to be sceptical
la religión no me dice nada	religion does nothing for me
ser ateo/a	to be an atheist
el ateísmo	atheism
ser agnóstico/a	to be an agnostic
el fanatismo religioso	religious fanaticism, bigotry
la (in)tolerancia religiosa	religious (in)tolerance
las matanzas sectarias	sectarian killings
el culto del diablo	devil worship
practicar el satanismo	to practise satanism

16.6 La muerte *Death*

morir	to die
fallecer	to die, pass away (more euphemistic)
después de morir	after death
el otro mundo	the other world, next world
los funerales	funeral
el cementerio	cemetery
el entierro	burial
enterrar	to bury
la cremación	cremation
incinerar	to cremate
el horno crematorio	crematorium
el luto	mourning
llorar la muerte de	to mourn the death of
la necrología	obituary
el testamento	will

La pobreza y el tercer mundo

un país tercermundista	a third-world country
los países en vías de desarrollo	the developing countries
los desvalidos	the underprivileged, the helpless
los desposeídos	the deprived, the have-nots
la pobreza	poverty

17.1 Los problemas humanos *Human problems*

17.1.1 Las condiciones económicas *Economic and health*
y sanitarias *conditions*

empobrecerse	to become poor / impoverished
el empobrecimiento	impoverishment
la desnutrición	malnutrition
estar desnutrido/a	to be malnourished
la mortalidad infantil	infant mortality
la miseria rural	rural deprivation
el hambre (f) endémica	endemic hunger / starvation
morir de inanición / hambre	to die of starvation
la marginación	marginalisation
estar marginado/a	to be marginalised
explotar	to exploit
sentirse explotado/a	to feel exploited
la lucha por la supervivencia cotidiana	the struggle for daily survival
la apatía	apathy
ser apático/a	to be apathetic
la desesperación	despair
encontrarse en condiciones cada vez más precarias	to be in an ever more precarious situation
las enfermedades relacionadas con la pobreza	poverty-related diseases
envejecer muy pronto	to age quickly
sufrir un irreversible deterioro en su forma de vivir	to suffer an irreversible decline in living conditions
ser analfabeto/a	to be illiterate
el analfabetismo	illiteracy
el ínfimo nivel de la educación	the abysmal level of education
mendigar	to beg
la desigualdad social	social inequality

obtener unos ingresos inferiores a la media de la renta per cápita	to receive an income below the per capita average
vivir por debajo del umbral de pobreza	to live below the poverty line
no llegar al final del mes	not to be able to manage until the end of the month
vivir en un estado de extrema necesidad	to live in a state of dire need
no tener recursos	to have no means / resources
depender de las limosnas	to depend on charity
robar para obtener víveres	to steal in order to obtain food
deber el alquiler	to owe the rent
desalojar	to evict
estar sin hogar	to be homeless
vivir en un cuchitril	to live in a hovel
las barriadas de chabolas	shanty towns
la chabola / el chamizo	shack, shanty, slum
el chabolismo	the problem of the *chabolas*
sustentar a siete u ocho niños	to support seven or eight children
el huérfano / la huérfana	orphan
el orfelinato	orphanage
ser carne de estadística	to be just a statistic, 'statistic fodder'
se acabó la esperanza	there's no more hope

17.1.2 Mejoras y soluciones

Improvements and solutions

la ayuda económica	economic aid
la organización caritativa	charity, charitable organisation
cobijar	to shelter, to house
la autosuficiencia alimenticia	self-sufficiency in food, ability to feed oneself
vivir de la tierra	to live off the land
abandonar el campo	to leave the countryside
desplazarse a la ciudad	to move to the city
compartir (con)	to share (with)
tener una auténtica política social hacia la pobreza	to have a real social policy towards poverty
el estado del bienestar	the welfare state
detectar manifestaciones de la pobreza	to detect signs of poverty
apadrinar a un niño	to sponsor a child
el comercio justo	fair trade

17.2 Los problemas económicos a nivel nacional

Economic problems at a national level

la deuda externa	foreign debt
el deudor	debtor
el acreedor	creditor
el préstamo	loan
reducir / suprimir / condonar la deuda del tercer mundo	to reduce / cancel third-world debt
atajar el crecimiento en espiral de la deuda del tercer mundo	to stem the spiralling growth of third-world debt
estar agobiado por el peso de la deuda externa	to be overwhelmed by the burden of foreign debt
el hundimiento económico	economic collapse
el crecimiento económico	economic growth
el Fondo Monetario Internacional	the International Monetary Fund
malgastar el dinero	to misspend money
la corrupción	corruption
los gobiernos corrompidos	corrupt governments
sobornar / cohechar	to bribe
el soborno / el cohecho	bribe, bribery
establecer severos planes de ajuste económico	to implement stringent plans for economic adjustment
un plan de austeridad económica	an economic austerity plan
un programa anti-inflacionario	an anti-inflationary programme
la inflación galopante	galloping inflation
una inflación que pasa ya del 300%	inflation already above 300%
mantener el caos a raya	to keep chaos at bay
el Banco Mundial	the World Bank
el sistema bancario mundial	the world banking system
las riquezas naturales	natural wealth / resources
aprovechar sus propios recursos	to benefit from one's own resources

17.3 Los efectos ecológicos *Ecological effects*

la desertización de la tierra	desertification of the land
la superpoblación	over-population
el agotamiento de la tierra	soil exhaustion
la sobreexplotación	over-exploitation
la sequía	drought
aridificarse	to become arid
la erosión	erosion
la deforestación	deforestation
la conservación de los bosques	conservation of forests
las zonas forestales	forested areas
la irrigación intensiva	intensive irrigation

You will find further relevant ecological vocabulary in Chapter 14.

www.redtercermundo.org.uy
www.bancomundial.org

18 La inmigración y el racismo

18.1 La inmigración — *Immigration*

inmigrar	to immigrate, i.e. to migrate in
el / la inmigrante	immigrant
emigrar	to emigrate, i.e. to migrate out
el / la emigrante	emigrant
el influjo de inmigrantes	influx of immigrants
la población inmigrante	immigrant population
el / la inmigrante 'sin papeles' } el / la inmigrante irregular }	illegal immigrant
proveniente(s) del Tercer Mundo / de los antiguos países comunistas / del Subsáhara	coming from the Third World / the former communist countries / sub-Saharan Africa
la Ley de Extranjería	(Spanish) Immigration Law
el país anfitrión	host country
el permiso de trabajo	work permit
el permiso de residencia	residence permit
el permiso / visado de salida	exit permit / visa
la libertad de movimiento	freedom of movement (i.e. of people, goods, etc.)
el centro de acogida	reception centre (for immigrants)
la mano de obra barata	cheap workforce
el empleo de baja remuneración	low-paid employment
la identidad cultural	cultural identity
integrarse en la sociedad	to integrate into society
el derecho a la ciudadanía	the right to citizenship
el derecho de voto	the right to vote
acelerar el proceso integrador	**to speed up the process of integration**
la concesión de la nacionalidad	the granting of nationality
tras cinco años de residencia continuada	after five years' continuous residency
el trabajador invitado	guest worker, immigrant worker
vivir fuera de su país de origen	to live outside one's country of origin
residir legalmente en ...	to reside legally in ...
la segunda generación	second generation
el matrimonio mixto	mixed marriage
solicitar / pedir asilo (político)	to seek (political) asylum
la solicitud de asilo	application for asylum
el solicitante de asilo político	asylum-seeker
la inmigración ilegal	illegal immigration

una riada creciente de inmigrantes clandestinos / ilegales	an increasing flow of illegal immigrants
agravar la escasez de viviendas	to aggravate the housing shortage
el refugiado / la refugiada de la persecución política	refugee from political persecution
la tortura	torture
repatriar	to repatriate

18.2 El racismo   *Racism*

18.2.1 La discriminación racial   *Racial discrimination*

el brote de racismo	outburst of racism
el racismo encubierto	hidden racism
el odio racista	race hatred
la agresión	aggression
discriminar	to discriminate
las desigualdades raciales	racial inequalities
un acto humillante	a humiliating act
humillar	to humiliate
la mano dura de la policía	police heavy-handedness
negar los derechos del hombre	to deny human rights
la vulneración de derechos individuales	infringement of individual rights
pisotear los principios morales	to trample on moral principles
un ciudadano de segunda categoría	a second-class citizen

18.2.2 Las actitudes racistas   *Racist attitudes*

la xenofobia	xenophobia
la extrema derecha	the extreme right
albergar sentimientos racistas	to harbour racist feelings
el movimiento neonazi	neo-Nazi movement
el sentimiento antijudío	anti-Jewish feeling
el antisemitismo	anti-Semitism
el choque de culturas	clash of cultures
fomentar el odio religioso	to stir up religious hatred
el ataque de carácter racista	racist attack
el atraco	mugging, hold-up
atracar	to mug, hold up
apalear	to beat up
el asesinato racista	racist murder
un incidente racista	a racist incident
un caso conocido de racismo	a known case of racism
una campaña de terror	a campaign of terror
una escalada de la violencia racista	an escalation of racist violence
una ley discriminatoria	a discriminatory law

estar / sentirse marginado/a	to be / feel marginalised
las cosas han empeorado	things have got worse
corregir una situación alarmante	to rectify an alarming situation
representar un amplio espectro social	to represent a wide spectrum of society
la incapacidad de vivir juntos	inability to live together

18.2.3 Vivir juntos — *Living together*

coexistir	to coexist
la minoría étnica	ethnic minority
preservar su identidad cultural	to retain one's cultural identity
el patrimonio cultural	cultural heritage
la eliminación de todas formas de racismo	elimination of all forms of racism
ser receptivo/a a la diversidad cultural	to be open to cultural diversity
las ventajas de vivir en una sociedad multirracial	the benefits of living in a multiracial society
vivir en una armonía racial	to live in racial harmony
tener respeto por la cultura de cada uno	to have respect for each other's culture

---

www.mtas.es
www.elpais.com/todo-sobre/tema/inmigracion/espana/27/-
www.inmigra.com

La guerra y la paz

19.1 El conducto de la guerra

The conduct of war

declarar la guerra	to declare war
emprender la guerra	to go to war
estar en guerra	to be at war
la guerra biológica	biological warfare
la guerra civil	civil war
la guerra fría	the cold war
la guerra de las galaxias	star wars
la guerra de nervios	war of nerves
la guerra química	chemical warfare
la guerra de trinchera	trench warfare
una guerra sangrienta	a bloody war
la lucha contra el terrorismo	the fight against terrorism
cuando estalló la guerra entre ...	when war broke out between ...
el aliado	ally
una potencia aliada	an allied power
el ultimátum	ultimatum
provocar una crisis	to provoke a crisis
prepararse para la confrontación / el enfrentamiento	to prepare for confrontation
desatar una guerra	to unleash a war
atacar	to attack
el ataque	attack
la agresión armada	armed agression
invadir	to invade
la invasión	invasion
aplastar las fuerzas enemigas	to crush the enemy forces
disparar	to fire (a gun)
incapacitar	to incapacitate
lesionar	to wound, injure
derrotar	to defeat
vencer	to beat
el botín	booty, spoils
el detenido / la detenida	detainee
el prisionero / la prisionera de guerra	prisoner of war
desterrar	to exile
el destierro	exile
la presencia militar	military presence
las superpotencias	superpowers
una fuerza potente	a powerful force

las sanciones internacionales	international sanctions
la pérdida de vidas humanas	the loss of human life
recibir órdenes	to receive orders
la Cruz Roja	Red Cross
la amenaza nuclear	the nuclear threat
el holocausto nuclear	nuclear holocaust
el genocidio	genocide

19.2 Las fuerzas armadas y el material bélico

The armed forces and military equipment

la jerarquía militar	military hierarchy
la máquina de guerra	war machine
el ejército	army
las tropas	troops
el servicio militar ⎱ 'la mili' (*coll*) ⎰	military service
el cuartel	barracks
la flota	fleet
la armada	navy
las fuerzas aéreas	air force
la brigada	brigade
el portaaviones	aircraft carrier
el avión de caza	fighter plane
el bombardero	bomber
el radar	radar
las tropas aerotransportadas	airborne troops
el destructor	destroyer
la fragata	frigate
el buque de guerra	warship
el tanque	tank
el dragaminas	minesweeper
el coche blindado	armoured car
la bomba	bomb
el cohete	rocket
el obús	shell
el gas nervioso	nerve gas
las armas químicas	chemical weapons
el armamento nuclear	nuclear armament
el sistema de misiles	missile system
La Fuerza de Acción Rápida (FAR)	Rapid Action Force
las armas de destrucción masiva	weapons of mass destruction

19.3 La paz — *Peace*

mantener la paz	to keep the peace
hacer las paces (con)	to make peace (with)
en tiempo de paz	in peacetime
el pacificador	peacekeeper
las fuerzas de pacificación	peacekeeping force
el apaciguamiento	appeasement
apaciguar	to appease
firmar un tratado	to sign a treaty
abogar por un cese de hostilidades	to call for an end to hostilities
aspirar a una solución negociada	to seek a negotiated solution
en los años de la posguerra	in the post-war years
disuadir	to deter
un arma (*f*) disuasiva	deterrent weapon
el movimiento de paz	peace movement
el pacifismo	pacifism
ser pacifista	to be a pacifist
la manifestación pacifista	peace demonstration
hacer una campaña antimilitarista	to carry out an anti-military campaign
el alto el fuego / el cese de hostilidades	ceasefire
'dad una oportunidad a la paz'	'give peace a chance'

www.terra.es/guerracivilespanola
www.guerracivil.org

NB: *There are many Spanish Civil War sites, some of which tend to be written from a very partisan point of view.*

20

Las relaciones internacionales

20.1 La diplomacia · *Diplomacy*

el protocolo	protocol
la diplomacia	diplomacy
diplomático/a	diplomatic
la ONU (Organización de las Naciones Unidas)	UN (United Nations)
la Asamblea General	the General Assembly
las relaciones hispano-británicas	Anglo-Spanish relations
un acuerdo bilateral	a bilateral agreement
la política exterior	foreign policy
los intereses nacionales	national interests
la presencia extranjera	foreign presence
el Ministerio de Asuntos Exteriores	Foreign Office
el Ministerio de Defensa	Ministry of Defence
el ministro / la ministra de Asuntos Exteriores	Foreign Secretary
la inversión extranjera	foreign investment
invertir	to invest
el indicador económico	economic indicator
la internacionalización de la economía	the internationalisation of the economy
la multinacional extranjera	foreign multinational (company)

20.2 La Unión Europea (UE) · *The European Union (EU)*

20.2.1 La organización y las instituciones · *The organisation and institutions*

la Unión Europea	European Union
el Tratado de Roma / Lisboa	Treaty of Rome / Lisbon
la Europa occidental	western Europe
ingresar en el antiguo Mercado Común	to join the former Common Market
solicitar la adhesión a la UE	to apply for membership of the EU
la apertura oficial de las negociaciones	the official opening of negotiations
el ingreso de España en la UE en 1986	the entry of Spain into the EU in 1986
el Pacto de Adhesión	Membership Pact

la integración en Europa	integration into Europe
las negociaciones	negotiations
negociar	to negotiate
el Parlamento Europeo	the European Parliament
el eurodiputado / la eurodiputada	member of the European Parliament (MEP)
el Consejo de Europa	Council of Europe
el Banco Europeo de Inversiones	the European Investment Bank
PIB (Producto Interior Bruto)	GNP (Gross National Product)
la competencia libre	free competition
el impuesto sobre el valor añadido (IVA)	Value Added Tax (VAT)
la política agrícola común (PAC)	common agricultural policy (CAP)
los países miembros	member countries
la unión aduanera	customs union
la homologación de instituciones	standardisation of institutions
el convenio	agreement
el funcionario / la funcionaria	civil servant
el pasaporte comunitario	Community passport
el sistema monetario europeo (SME)	European monetary system (EMS)
una moneda común	a common currency
el estreno del euro en el 2002	the launch of the euro in 2002
la eurozona	Eurozone, Euroland
la armonización de las políticas económicas	harmonisation of economic policies
el período transitorio	transition period
el arancel	customs tariff
el desarme arancelario	removal of tariff barriers
firmar un acuerdo de cooperación	to sign a cooperation agreement
la ampliación de la UE	expansion of the EU
basta ya con los veintisiete	27's enough (relating to the EU)

20.2.2 Los efectos de la adhesión a la UE

The effects of joining the EU

hacer frente al desafío de la adhesión	to face up to the challenge of membership
el desarrollo regional	regional development
el aumento de las importaciones / exportaciones	increase in imports / exports
la competencia europea	European competition
renunciar a una parte de su soberanía	to give up a degree of sovereignty
eliminar las barreras	to break down barriers
la libertad de la circulación de mercancías (personas, capitales)	freedom of movement of goods (people, capital)
la modernización de estructuras	modernisation of structures
modernizar	to modernise

una mayor renta agraria	a greater agricultural income
compartir las aguas pesqueras	to share fishing waters
la flota pesquera española	the Spanish fishing fleet
el desarrollo industrial	industrial development
la ampliación del mercado nacional	increasing the national market
el rendimiento exigido por la UE	performance required by the EU
la compañía exportadora / importadora	export / import company
el incremento del coste de la vida	increase in the cost of living
protegerse del impacto del cambio	to protect oneself from the effects of change
adaptarse a la competencia comunitaria	to adapt to Community-wide competition
la subida general de precios alimenticios	general rise in food prices
el consumidor español	the Spanish consumer
un abaratamiento para el consumidor	a price cut for the consumer
ampliar sus gamas de productos	to widen one's range of products
homologar los niveles de calidad	to standardise quality levels
la supresión de barreras proteccionistas	the abolition of protectionist barriers
las barreras aduaneras	customs barriers
el movimiento de trabajadores	the movement of workers
una mayor estabilidad	a greater stability
la sobreexplotación de los recursos del mar	over-exploitation of the sea's resources
la conservación y la gestión de los recursos	conservation and management of resources
la estrategia energética común	common energy strategy
la igualdad de oportunidades para todos los ciudadanos europeos	equality of opportunity for all European citizens
los retos para el futuro	challenges for the future
añorar la vuelta de la peseta	to long for the return of the peseta
ser euroescéptico/a	to be (a) Eurosceptic
estar gobernado desde Bruselas	to be governed from Brussels

20.3 La OTAN

NATO

la Organización del Tratado del Atlántico del Norte	North Atlantic Treaty Organisation
el secretario general	general secretary
permanecer en la Alianza Atlántica	to remain in the Atlantic Alliance
integrarse en la estructura militar de mando	to become part of the military command structure
la situación de seguridad	the security situation
los aliados	the allies
la defensa de Europa	the defence of Europe

la pérdida de la libertad de acción	loss of freedom of action
los objetivos militares	military objectives
en la época de la guerra fría	at the time of the Cold War
la carrera de armamentos	the arms race
los países no alineados	the non-aligned countries
el valor estratégico de España	Spain's strategic value
la importancia militar	military importance
supeditar la libertad de acción a la OTAN	to subordinate freedom of action to NATO
firmar un acuerdo mutuo de defensa	to sign a mutual defence agreement
deshacerse de las bases norteamericanas	to get rid of American bases
la presencia militar	military presence
la cumbre	summit (meeting)
el equilibrio militar	military balance
el desequilibrio	imbalance
el presupuesto defensivo	the defence budget

20.4 Gibraltar

el Peñón / la Roca	the Rock (i.e. Gibraltar)
gibraltareño/a	Gibraltarian
el llanito / la llanita (*coll*)	Gibraltarian
el contencioso de Gibraltar	the argument over Gibraltar
la colonia británica	British colony
la descolonización	decolonisation
descolonizar	to decolonise
resolver el problema de Gibraltar	to solve the Gibraltar problem
abordar las cuestiones de la soberanía	to tackle the questions of sovereignty
la autodeterminación	self-determination
la devolución de Gibraltar a España	the return of Gibraltar to Spain
ceder el Peñón	to give up the Rock
recuperar Gibraltar	to regain / get Gibraltar back
demostrar una capacidad de compromiso	to show a capacity for compromise
una soberanía compartida	shared sovereignty
las discusiones concluyeron sin acuerdo	the discussions ended without an agreement
los gibraltareños no quieren someterse a la soberanía española	the Gibraltarians don't want to submit to Spanish rule
a través de los canales diplomáticos ordinarios	through normal diplomatic channels
la importancia estratégica	strategic importance
la seguridad del Estrecho	the security of the Strait
el paraíso fiscal	tax haven
considerar los aspectos militares y estratégicos	to consider the military and strategic aspects

20.4 Gibraltar   107

levantar restricciones	to lift restrictions
abrir la verja	to open the frontier gate (between Spain and Gibraltar)
la apertura de la verja	the opening of the frontier gate (between Spain and Gibraltar)
la frontera terrestre	the land frontier
los aduaneros españoles se ponen en paro técnico	the Spanish Customs work to rule

www.un.org/spanish
www.europarl.es

La política

21.1 La democracia

Democracy

21.1.1 El sistema parlamentario

The parliamentary system

el Parlamento	Parliament
las Cortes	(Spanish) Parliament
la Cámara	Chamber
el Congreso de los Diputados	the Congress of Deputies (Spanish lower house)
la Cámara de los Comunes	House of Commons
la Cámara de los Lores	House of Lords
el presidente del gobierno	president, prime minister
el primer ministro / la primera ministra	prime minister
el gabinete	cabinet
el partido	party
los máximos dirigentes del partido	the top party leaders
el / la líder	leader
bajo el liderazgo de Aznar	under the leadership of Aznar
el gobierno encabezado por Zapatero	the government headed by Zapatero
gobernar	to govern
un gobierno de izquierdas / derechas	a left-wing / right-wing government
derechista (*n* / *adj*)	right-wing, right-winger
izquierdista (*n* / *adj*)	left-wing, left-winger
el ala (*f*) derecha del partido	the right wing of the party
el comunismo	communism
comunista	communist
el / la comunista	communist (*n*)
el socialismo	socialism
socialista	socialist
el / la socialista	socialist (*n*)
el gobierno laborista	Labour government
el partido centrista	centre party
el conservadurismo	conservatism
conservador(a)	conservative
el conservador / la conservadora	conservative (*n*)
el poder político	political power
el grupo político	political group
la agrupación política	political grouping
el político / la política	politician
la política	politics / policy
la política verde	green politics

la clase media alta / baja	the upper / lower middle class
con el apoyo de la clase obrera	with working-class support
apoyar	to support
el debate	debate
el discurso	speech
la réplica	reply
la polémica	discussion, argument, polemic
por motivos políticos	for political motives / reasons
la oposición	the opposition
la actitud política	political attitude
mantener las fuerzas de orden público	to maintain the forces of public order
lograr el objetivo de sacar a España adelante	to achieve the objective of moving Spain forward
los derechos humanos	human rights
salvaguardar las libertades y los derechos del pueblo	to safeguard the freedoms and rights of the people
mantener vivo el sistema democrático	to keep the democratic system alive

21.1.2 Las elecciones — *Elections*

elegir	to elect
las elecciones generales	general election
las elecciones autonómicas	regional government / *autonomía* elections
la campaña electoral	election campaign
el electorado	electorate
ganar 100 escaños	to win 100 (parliamentary) seats
el voto	vote
votar (por los socialistas)	to vote (for the socialists)
las urnas	ballot boxes
acudir a las urnas	to go to the polls
el referéndum	referendum
el / la portavoz	spokesperson
el sondeo	opinion poll
el boicot	boycott
boicotear	to boycott

21.2 La dictadura — *Dictatorship*

el régimen	régime
el franquismo	Francoism, politics of the Franco régime
en la época franquista	in Franco's time
el dictador	dictator
la dictadura	dictatorship

el Caudillo	fascist leader (esp. with reference to Franco)
el fascismo	fascism
fascista	fascist (adj)
el / la fascista	fascist (n)
el / la facha (*coll*)	(derogatory slang term for) fascist
ultraderechista	extreme right-wing
el golpe de estado	*coup d'état*
el golpismo	*coup* mentality
el / la golpista	one who takes part in a *coup*
el gobierno títere	puppet government

21.3 La violencia política
Political violence

21.3.1 Los responsables
The perpetrators

el / la terrorista	terrorist
la organización terrorista	terrorist organisation
el grupo terrorista	terrorist group
el guerrillero / la guerrillera	guerrilla
la guerra de guerrillas	guerrilla warfare
los rebeldes	the rebels
el / la simpatizante	sympathiser
el grupo separatista	separatist group
ETA (Euskadi Ta Askatasuna)	ETA (Basque separatist group)
etarra	member of, or to do with, ETA
una célula del Al-Qaeda	an Al-Qaeda cell

21.3.2 Sus razones y objetivos
Their reasons and objectives

derrocar el gobierno	to bring down the government
la corrupción de los políticos	political corruption
corromper	to corrupt
corrompido/a	corrupt
la ley del patrón	the law of the rich owner / boss
luchar por la independencia	to struggle / fight for independence

21.3.3 Sus métodos
Their methods

protestar	to protest
la sublevación	uprising
la revolución	revolution
revolucionario/a	revolutionary
los disturbios callejeros	street riots
el cuartelazo	military uprising, army *coup*
el golpe militar	military *coup*

las operaciones guerrilleras	guerrilla operations
la violencia terrorista	terrorist violence
el atentado terrorista	terrorist outrage
el atentado con bomba	bomb outrage
secuestrar	to kidnap
el coche bomba	car bomb
el hombre / la mujer bomba	suicide bomber
entregar su vida (por)	to give up one's life (for)
la bomba de relojería	booby-trap bomb
el explosivo Semtex	Semtex explosive
volar un tren	to blow up a train
asesinar	to murder
el asesinato	murder
quitarle la vida a alguien	to take someone's life
mutilar	to maim
lesionar	to injure
herir	to wound
degollar a alguien	to behead sb / cut sb's throat
rescatar	to ransom
el rescate	ransom
el atentado	outrage / attempt on someone's life
el asesinato político	political assassination / murder
hundir el país en la guerra civil	to plunge the country into civil war
las matanzas colectivas	mass killings
la masacre sangrienta	bloody massacre
ahogar(se) en sangre	to drown in blood
matar por matar	to kill for the sake of killing
crear continuos conflictos	to create continual conflicts
la canción de protesta	protest song
'el pueblo unido jamás será vencido'	'the people united will never be defeated'
el alto el fuego	cease-fire

21.3.4 Sus víctimas

Their victims

el / la víctima	victim
la desaparición	disappearance
tomar a una persona como rehén	to take sb hostage
los rehenes detenidos en Iraq	the hostages held in Iraq
estar sobrecogido/a por el terror	to be cowed by terror
los desaparecidos violentamente	those who have disappeared by force

21.3.5 Las contramedidas

Counter-measures

los organismos internacionales de derechos humanos	international human rights organisations
evitar una guerra civil	to avoid a civil war
firmar una tregua	to sign a truce

romper una tregua	to break a truce
la ruptura de una tregua	the breaking of a truce
desactivar una bomba	to defuse a bomb
el artificiero / experto en desactivar explosivos	bomb disposal expert
tener el apoyo del gobierno	to have the support of the government

21.4 La monarquía
The monarchy

21.4.1 La Familia Real
The Royal Family

el / la monarca	monarch
el soberano / la soberana	sovereign
los Reyes de España	King and Queen of Spain
el Príncipe de Asturias	Prince of Asturias
la Infanta Elena	Princess Elena
la corona española	the Spanish crown
la Familia Real	Royal Family
la Zarzuela	home of Spanish royal family
el presupuesto anual	annual budget
el Jefe de Estado	Head of State
la coronación	coronation
las obligaciones oficiales	official duties
reinar	to reign
el reino	kingdom, realm
durante el reinado de	during the reign of
la Constitución de 1978	the 1978 Constitution
el sistema constitucional	constitutional system
el jefe de las Fuerzas Armadas	chief of the armed forces
mantenerse por encima de la política cotidiana	to remain above everyday politics
cumplir con su deber	to fulfil one's duty
las cuestiones protocolarias	matters of protocol
tener sangre real	to have royal blood

21.4.2 En pro y en contra de la monarquía
For and against the monarchy

ser monárquico/a	to be a monarchist
desde un punto de vista (anti-) monárquico ...	from a(n anti-)monarchist point of view
estar en pro / en contra de la monarquía	to be for / against the monarchy
gozar del privilegio	to enjoy privilege
privilegiado/a	privileged

gozar del poder hereditario	to enjoy hereditary power
disfrutar de la riqueza heredada	to enjoy inherited (unearned) wealth
deberían trabajar como cualquier hijo de vecino	they should have to work like any other citizen
pagar los impuestos	to pay taxes
ofrecer estabilidad	to offer stability
gozar de un prestigio sin parangón	to enjoy unequalled prestige
hacerse querer por todos	to be loved by all
el Rey Juan Carlos ...	King Juan Carlos ...
... fue el protagonista de la transición democrática	... was the leader of the transition to democracy
... desempeñó un papel primordial en	... played a fundamental role in
el cambio hacia la democracia	the change to democracy

21.5 Las autonomías — *The self-governing regions*

el regionalismo	regionalism
el gobierno regional	regional government
el deseo autonómico	desire for regional government
el autogobierno	self-government
la Comunidad Autónoma	self-governing region (of Spain)
reconocer el derecho a la autonomía	to recognise the right to self-government
tener una lengua propia	to have one's own language
suscitar expectativas	to awaken expectations
esto no supone una panacea para ...	this does not imply a panacea for ...
crear conflictos sociales	to create social conflict
crear más burocracia	to create more bureaucracy
se tiende a una Europa sin fronteras	there is a tendency to a Europe without frontiers
la lengua catalana	the Catalan language
la Generalitat	Catalan Parliament
los vascos	the Basques
el País Vasco ⎫ Euskadi ⎬	the Basque Country
el euskera	Basque (language)

---

www.casareal.es
www.elpais.es/diario/autonomias.html

The main political parties:
www.psoe.es
www.pp.es
www.izquierda-unida.es

You can easily find other parties via a search engine.

La economía y los negocios

22.1 La economía

The economy

22.1.1 A nivel gubernamental

At government level

la economía dirigida	planned economy
la economía del mercado	market economy
el centro bancario y financiero mundial	world banking and financial centre
el sector público	public sector
el sector privado	private sector
privatizar	to privatise
la privatización	privatisation
fomentar el capital privado	to encourage private capital
nacionalizar	to nationalise
la nacionalización	nationalisation
globalizar	to globalise
la globalización	globalisation
la mundialización	extension worldwide, internationalisation
Hacienda	Treasury, Exchequer
el ministro / la ministra de Hacienda	Chancellor of the Exchequer
la deuda nacional	national debt
la balanza de pagos	balance of payments
subvencionar	to subsidise
la subvención	subsidy
las actividades económicas	economic activities
el despegue de la economía española	the lift-off of the Spanish economy
el mercado de cambio de monedas	foreign exchange market
tras años de estancamiento	after years of stagnation
el presupuesto	budget
el consumidor / la consumidora	consumer
la tasa de cambio	exchange rate
la devaluación	devaluation
devaluar / revaluar el peso argentino	to devalue / revalue the Argentinian peso
las divisas extranjeras	foreign exchange, currency
la estadística	statistic(s)
bruto/a	gross
neto/a	net
combatir la inflación	to combat inflation

la tasa de la inflación	inflation rate
la espiral inflacionista	the spiral of inflation
invertir capital en España	to invest capital in Spain
la inversión	investment
la libre competencia	free competition
el mercado libre	free market
estar sujeto/a a las fuerzas del mercado	to be subject to market forces

NB:

la banca	the banks (collectively), banking
el banco	bank (building or company)
los movimientos bancarios	bank movements
la fluctuación de los tipos de interés	interest rate fluctuation
el alza (f) / la baja en los tipos de interés	rise / fall in interest rates
la crisis económica	economic crisis
la recesión	recession
la entidad financiera	financial institution
el descenso de la demanda	downturn in demand
el crecimiento más lento	slower growth
la contracción del sector constructor	contraction of the building sector
impedir el hundimiento de la economía	to prevent the collapse of the economy

22.1.2 A nivel personal — *On a personal level*

el consumismo	consumerism
la sociedad consumista	the consumer society
los bienes de consumo	consumer goods
el poder adquisitivo	purchasing power
la cesta de la compra	shopping basket
el ahorro	savings
la Caja de Ahorros	savings bank
ahorrar	to save
la Bolsa	Stock Exchange
el / la agente de Bolsa	stockbroker
las acciones	shares
el / la accionista	shareholder
el préstamo	loan
prestar	to lend
la hipoteca	mortgage
hipotecar	to mortgage
el impuesto sobre la renta	income tax
el impuesto sobre el valor añadido (IVA)	value added tax (VAT)
la plusvalía	appreciation, capital gains tax
la tarjeta de crédito	credit card
el cajero automático	automatic cash dispenser
pedir el saldo	to ask for a balance statement
la suplantación de la identidad	identity theft
el fraude de las tarjetas de crédito	credit card fraud

22.2 Los negocios   *Business*

la empresa	firm, company
la (empresa) subsidiaria	subsidiary, branch
la entidad	company, organisation
los recursos	resources
el beneficio	profit
el margen de beneficio	profit margin
un negocio rentable	a profitable business
la renta	income, revenue
la rentabilidad	profitability
la pérdida	loss
la contabilidad	accounting
el / la contable	accountant
el acreedor	creditor
la cooperativa	cooperative
el convenio	agreement, accord
la venta al detalle / al por menor	retail sale
la venta al por mayor	wholesale
el contrato multimillonario	multimillion contract
las posibilidades de desarrollo	development possibilities
incrementar la productividad	to increase productivity
mantener la liquidez	to maintain liquidity, solvency
las cifras de exportación	export figures
la importación	import
financiar un proyecto	to finance a project
la fusión de dos empresas	merger of two companies
el pago	payment
las pérdidas	losses
la mercancía	goods, merchandise
la planificación	planning
planificar	to plan
el riesgo	risk
arriesgar	to risk
la venta a plazos	sale by instalments

You will find further associated vocabulary in Chapter 6.

---

www.bancomundial.org
www.bde.es
www.meh.es
www.infobolsa.es

23

Amigos algo falsos y muy falsos

Many Spanish words of almost identical appearance to their English equivalents also have much the same meaning. Some, however, although they may share one or more meanings, are used more commonly with a different sense, as in Section 23.1. Some other words have a totally different meaning, which could even lead you into embarrassing situations. These latter, in Section 23.2, are known as 'false friends'. So pay close attention to these lists!

23.1 ¡Cuidadito! — *Be a bit careful!*

el aborto	abortion (but can mean 'miscarriage')
abortar	to abort, have a miscarriage
absolutamente	absolutely (but often 'absolutely not')
en absoluto	not at all, absolutely not
adecuado	suitable
admirar	to surprise, astonish
agitar	to wave (arms, etc.)
aguardar	to wait (for)
alterar(se)	to make / get upset, angry
anciano/a	(applied to people) old person
anticipar(se)	to bring / take place early
antiguo	ancient, but also former, one-time
asistir (a)	to be present at, attend (NOT 'to assist')
la asistencia	attendance (rather than 'assistance')
la batería	drums (in band)
bruto	coarse, rough, uncouth; gross (weight, etc.)
la cacerola	saucepan
el canguro	baby-sitter
colapsar	to jam, disrupt (e.g. traffic)
el colapso	jam, blockage
la comisión	committee
la comodidad	comfort
completo	full (hotel, bus, etc.)
la conferencia	lecture
el cristal	pane of glass, window pane
crudo	raw, uncooked, untreated
cuestión	question (to be discussed, rather than asked)
la desgracia	misfortune, bad luck
por desgracia	unfortunately

divertir(se)	to amuse / be amused
efectivamente / en efecto	in fact, indeed, actually
la época	period of time, season
el establo	cowshed
fatal	dreadful, awful, ghastly
la frase	sentence (NOT 'phrase')
genial	inspired, brilliant
el genio	disposition, nature; <u>bad</u> temper
ignorar	not to know, to be ignorant of
el infante / la infanta	prince / princess
la memoria	memory (mechanism)
la moneda	coin; currency
la oración	prayer
particular	private
la propaganda	advertising
la ración	portion, helping (of food)
real	royal
el régimen (*NB*: los regímenes)	diet
registrar	to search, inspect (baggage, etc.)
regular (*adj*)	so-so (health, quality, etc.)
solicitar	ask for, request; apply for (job)
suceder	to happen (only 'succeed' in sense of 'come after')

23.2 ¡Mucho cuidado!   *Be very careful!*

acomodar(se)	to make (oneself) comfortable
acostar(se)	to put / go to bed, lie down
actual	present (in time)
actualmente	at present, now
afrontar	to face up to
avisar	to warn
la bala	bullet
balancear(se)	to rock, sway
el balón	(large) ball, e.g. football
bizarro	brave, gallant
el campo	field, country (as opposed to town)
la carpeta	folder, portfolio
casual	chance (*adj*)
casualmente / por casualidad	by chance
la casualidad	chance, coincidence
el c(h)rismas	Christmas <u>card</u>
el collar	necklace
el compromiso	commitment, engagement; predicament
comprometerse	to commit oneself; get into a predicament
concretar(se)	to make / become more specific

el delito	crime, offence
el disgusto	annoyance, displeasure
embarazarse	to become pregnant
embarazada	pregnant
energético (*adj*)	to do with energy, e.g. *crisis energética* (use *enérgico* for person, etc.)
eventual	fortuitous, dependent upon circumstances
el éxito	success
fastidiar(se)	to annoy / get annoyed
el fastidio	annoyance
el flan	crème caramel
la gana	desire, wish
tener ganas de	to wish to, feel like (doing sth)
gentil	elegant, graceful
el gusto	pleasure, delight; taste
honesto	decent, chaste
honrado	honest, honourable
el idioma	language
jubilarse	to retire
largo	long
la letra	letter of alphabet, handwriting, words of song
loco	mad
molestar	to annoy, irritate
la molestia	annoyance, irritation
el nudo	knot
el obsequio	gift, present
la parcela	plot of land
el pariente / la parienta	relative, relation
pinchar	to prick, puncture
pisar	to tread, trample
el preservativo	condom
pretender	to seek to, try to; claim
el profesor / la profesora	teacher
quitar(se)	to take away, remove, take off
el rato	(short) while
recordar	to remember
el refrán	proverb, saying
la renta	income
revolver	to stir, mix up, turn round / over
la ropa	clothes
sano	healthy
el talón	heel (of shoe); cheque, cheque stub
la tinta	ink; dye
la tormenta	storm

¡Escoge la palabra correcta!

You need to take great care when selecting the Spanish equivalent of these English words.

24.1 ¡Cuidado!	***Careful!***

to appear
| come into sight | aparecer |
| seem | parecer |

to apply
| for job | solicitar, pedir |
| substance (to) | aplicar (a) |

to argue
| quarrel | reñir |
| reason | argüir |

to ask
a question	preguntar
sb for sth	pedir algo a alguien
sb to do sth	pedir a alguien que haga algo

to become
+ n	hacerse, convertirse en
+ occupation	hacerse, llegar a ser
+ adj	ponerse; hacerse (*implies effort*)
or make verb from adj	e.g. independizarse (*become independent*)

both
| referring to two people or objects | ambos/as, los / las dos |
| both ... and ... | tanto ... como ... |

to burn
| consume or damage by fire | quemar |
| be on fire | arder |

to care
look after	cuidar
care / worry about	preocuparse por, interesarse por
take care	tener cuidado

care (n)
    anxiety   **la inquietud**

to come   **venir**
For come in / out / up / down, etc, see also under 'go'.

to drive
    drive a vehicle   **conducir**
    drive somewhere   **ir en coche**
    drive + adj   **volver** (e.g. volver loco – *drive mad*)

to enjoy
    have use / benefit of   **gozar**
    (circumstances, health, etc.)
    take delight in   **gustar** (e.g. ¿te gustó la película? –
                                     did you enjoy the film?)

    enjoy oneself   **divertirse**
                                  pasarlo bien

to fail
    be a flop, not succeed   **fracasar**
    crops, machinery, etc.   **fallar**
    in obligation, duty, etc.   **faltar**
    an exam   **suspender**
    fail to do sth   **dejar de hacer algo**
There are numerous other idiomatic uses: check in the dictionary!

to get
*This is a multipurpose word in English! The best tip is to find another English
word which expresses the meaning of 'get' and use the Spanish equivalent.*
    obtain   **obtener, conseguir**
    receive   **recibir**
    become + adj   **ponerse**
    or convert adj to v, e.g. *cansarse* – to get tired, *mojarse* – to get wet
    go and get   **ir por**

to go   **ir**
    go / come in(to)   **entrar (en)**
    go / come out (of)   **salir (de)**
    go / come up   **subir**
    go / come down   **bajar**
    go / come across   **cruzar, atravesar**
    go / come back   **volver**
    go / come by   **pasar**
    go away   **irse, marcharse, alejarse**
See also Section 24.2.4 below.

to know

know a fact, know that ...	saber (que)
know how to	saber + *inf*
know / be acquainted with a person / place	conocer
NOT to know (a fact / that ...)	ignorar

last

in series	último
previous (e.g. last Monday)	pasado

to leave

go off / away	irse, marcharse
train, plane, etc.	salir (de)
leave (the house, work, etc.)	salir (de casa, del trabajo, etc.)
allow to remain	dejar
abandon	abandonar

to let

rent out	alquilar
permit, let sth happen	dejar (+ *inf* or *subj*), permitir (+ *subj*), que + *pres subj*

to listen

(usually)	escuchar
to the radio, CDs, etc.	oír

to love

a person	querer, amar
an activity, food, etc.	encantar (e.g. me encanta – *I love it*)
fall in love (with)	enamorarse (de)
be in love (with)	estar enamorado/a (de)

to look

look at	mirar
look for, have a look for	buscar
seem	parecer
look like, resemble	parecerse a

look (n)

act of looking	la mirada
appearance	el aspecto
fashion	la moda, el estilo

to manage
    manage to   conseguir, lograr + *inf*
    a tool, etc.   manejar
    a company   dirigir, gestionar

to move
    (general)   mover (*trans*), moverse (*intrans*)
    move house   mudarse de casa

to order
    command   mandar, ordenar
    request (e.g. purchase)   pedir, encargar
    in restaurant   pedir

order (n)
    for purchase or food   el pedido
    command   <u>la</u> orden
    succession, arrangement   <u>el</u> orden

to put
    (general)   poner
    place   colocar
    put into   meter (en)

quite
    completely   totalmente, completamente
    rather, somewhat   bastante, algo, un poco
    not quite   no del todo

to reflect
    reflect light   reflejar
    think   reflexionar

to run
    action of running   correr
    run an organisation, etc. dirigir
    in a particular direction:
        run up   subir corriendo
        run down   bajar corriendo
        run in(to)   entrar corriendo (en)
        run out (from)   salir corriendo (de)

to sit
    sit down (i.e. action)   sentarse
    be sitting / seated (state) estar sentado/a

sorry

when you interrupt or unintentionally hurt sb	¡perdón!
to apologise emphatically, generally express regret, be sorry about	sentir, lamentar
to be (very) sorry that …	sentir (mucho) que + *subj*

to stand

stand up	levantarse, ponerse de pie
be standing (if bodily position is of importance)	estar de pie
otherwise	estar parado
tolerate, put up with	aguantar, soportar

to stop

bring / come to a halt	parar(se), detener(se)
stop doing sth	dejar / terminar de hacer algo
cease (e.g. rain)	cesar
prevent sb from doing sth	impedir que alguien haga algo

to succeed

be successful	tener éxito
succeed in (doing)	conseguir / lograr + *inf*
be next in succession to	suceder a

to take

general	tomar
take hold of, catch	coger

Warning: this verb has vulgar sexual connotations in most of Spanish America – use tomar!

occupy	ocupar
take sb or sth somewhere (i.e. lead, transport)	llevar
take out (from)	sacar (de)

then

next	luego, entonces
at that time	entonces
so, in that case	pues, entonces

time

concept or duration	el tiempo
occasion	la vez
time of day	la hora
period / span of time	la época
short period of time / while	el rato
to have a good time	divertirse, pasarlo bien

to try
    endeavour to   tratar de, intentar, procurar
    try out, try on (i.e. test, sample)   probar

to turn (as intrans v)
    revolve   girar
    change direction   volver
    turn round   volverse, dar la vuelta
    turn into (become)   convertirse en, transformarse en
    turn + adj   volverse, ponerse

to walk
    action of walking   andar
    to go for a walk   pasearse, dar un paseo
    in a particular direction:
      walk up   subir andando
      walk down   bajar andando
      walk in(to)   entrar andando (en)
      walk out (of)   salir andando (de)

to wipe
    clean   limpiar
    dry   secar, enjugar

to work
    do work   trabajar
    function   funcionar

work (n)
    job, the work you do   el trabajo
    work of art   la obra
    road / building works   las obras

24.2 Sinónimos para palabras corrientes

Synonyms for common words

We are all inclined to use common, general-purpose words such as 'to be', 'to have', 'lots of', when we could and should be more precise. Here are some alternative suggestions. However, a word of warning: some 'synonyms' might not be synonymous with <u>all</u> meanings of a particular word, and might have a particular nuance, hence the reason for including some examples to help you decide.

24.2.1 Ser / Estar

To be

Be aware first of all of the differences between **ser** and **estar**, which you will find fully explained in any grammar book.

Estar
* *be in a place, position or state (talking of people):* **encontrarse, hallarse**

Cuando llamaste me encontraba / me hallaba bajo la ducha	When you called I was in the shower
El perro se encontraba / se hallaba acostado en la huerta	The dog was lying in the garden
Loli se encontraba enferma aquel día	Loli was ill that day

* *be in a place, talking of objects or towns, cities etc:* **encontrarse, hallarse, situarse,** *and rather more sophisticatedly,* **ubicarse**

Salamanca se encuentra / se halla / se sitúa / se ubica en el río Tormes
Salamanca se encuentra ubicada en el río Tormes
} Salamanca is on the river Tormes

* *be in a state, usually after an action (not necessarily expressed):* **quedar**

La ciudad quedaba en ruinas	The town was (left) in ruins
Ana quedó perpleja	Ana was puzzled

Ser
* *be considered:* **considerarse**

Aquella pista de esquí se considera la más peligrosa	That ski slope is the most dangerous
Pepe se considera muy listo	Pepe thinks he is very clever

24.2.2 Hay

There is / there are

- **se encuentra(n)**: *there is / are to be found*

- **se ve(n)**: *there is / are to be seen*

Se encuentran / ven muchos
 edificios históricos en esta ciudad
Se veía una larga cola delante
 de la puerta

There are lots of historic buildings
 in this town
There was a long queue in
 front of the door

- **existir**: *to exist*

Existe un gran número de remedios
 para este problema

There are lots of solutions to
 this problem

24.2.3 Poseer, etc.

Have, have got

- *possess, own*: **poseer**

Poseo un ordenador muy rápido
Mi hermana posee un perro
 encantador

I've got a very fast computer
My sister's got a delightful dog

- *suffer from*: **sufrir de**, **padecer de**

La pobre sufría / padecía de una
 artritis severa

The poor woman had severe arthritis

24.2.4 Ir, etc.

To go / come

- *to a place*: **dirigirse a**, **viajar**, **desplazarse a** *(implies effort or travel)*

Jaime se dirigió hacia la puerta
Viajo / me desplazo cada día desde
 Segovia a Madrid

Jaime went / came towards the door
I go / come from Segovia to Madrid
 each day

- *go away*: **irse**, *but also* **marcharse**, **alejarse**, **largarse**

¿Cuándo te marchas / te vas?

When are you going (away)?

- *go / move away*: **alejarse** *(tends to emphasise increasing distance;
 it's derived from* **lejos***)*

El tren se alejaba de la estación

The train was going / moving away
 from the station

- *go / move away:* **largarse** (*often gives the idea of 'clearing off!'*)

¡Lárgate!   Off you go!

- *go / come towards, approach:* **acercarse**, **aproximarse** (*often but not necessarily more abstract*)

El tren se acercaba   The train was coming / approaching
Se aproxima el invierno   Winter is coming

24.2.5 Mucho / mucha / muchos / muchas   *A lot, much, lots, many*

Try also:
una gran cantidad de   a large quantity of
una cantidad enorme de   a huge / vast quantity of
grandes cantidades de   large quantities of
cantidades enormes de   huge / vast quantities of
un montón de / montones de   a heap of, heaps of
                                               (slightly more colloquial)

una multitud de   a multitude of
una muchedumbre de   a great number of
un sinnúmero de   no end of, a great many
miles / millares de   thousands of
toneladas de   tons of

24.2.6 Muy   *Very*

- *You can often use the suffix* **-ísimo** *on an adjective:*

caro – carísimo   very / extremely expensive
rico – riquísimo   very / extremely rich

Don't forget that these may also be converted into an adverb:
estupidísimamente   very / extremely stupidly

- *Use:*

extremadamente:
extremadamente generoso   extremely generous
enormemente:
enormemente feo   enormously ugly

and other adverbs which suggest an extreme or superlative:
importantemente, notablemente, *etc.*

25 Algunos verbos útiles

The following is a selection of – mainly abstract – verbs which cannot be listed under particular topic headings but are very useful in written and spoken argument.

abolish	eliminar, suprimir
accuse	acusar
get accustomed to	acostumbrarse a
achieve	conseguir
acknowledge (recognise)	reconocer
act	actuar (*in theatre*); actuar, obrar (*do sth*)
add	añadir
admit	admitir (*all senses*); confesar (*confess*)
advise	aconsejar
afford	costear
agree to	consentir en, quedar en
agree with	ponerse / estar de acuerdo con
allow	permitir
alter	cambiar
annoy	fastidiar, enojar
apologise	disculparse
appreciate	apreciar (*most senses*); valorar (*value*)
approve	aprobar
assist	ayudar
assume	asumir
assure	asegurar
attempt	intentar, probar
attract	atraer
avenge (oneself)	vengar(se)
avoid	evitar
balance	equilibrar
bear (endure)	aguantar
behave	comportarse
betray	traicionar
blame	culpar
boast	jactarse
borrow	pedir prestado
cancel	anular, cancelar, suprimir
cheat (deceive)	burlar
check	comprobar
choose	escoger, elegir
command	mandar, ordenar
compel	obligar

complain	quejarse, lamentarse
compose	componer
conclude	concluir
confess	confesar
confuse	confundir
congratulate (on)	felicitar (por)
dare (to)	atreverse a, osar
deal (with something)	tratar de
decrease, diminish	disminuir
demand	exigir, reivindicar
deny	negar
depend (on)	depender (de)
deserve	merecer
despise	despreciar
develop	desarrollar
disagree	no estar de acuerdo, oponerse (object)
disagree	reñir, discutir (quarrel)
disappoint	decepcionar
disgust	dar asco
distrust	desconfiar de, recelar
emphasise	subrayar
endure	aguantar
envy	envidiar
excuse	perdonar
fail	fracasar
favour	favorecer
fear	temer
fight (for)	luchar (por)
forbid	prohibir
foresee	prever
forget	olvidar
forgive	perdonar
frighten	asustar, dar un susto a
fulfil	cumplir
govern	gobernar
grumble (about)	protestar (de)
hasten	apresurarse (*intrans*), acelerar (*trans*)
hate	odiar, aborrecer
hesitate	dudar, vacilar
hinder	impedir, estorbar
imagine	imaginarse, figurarse
improve	mejorar
increase	aumentar (*trans*), aumentarse (*intrans*)
influence	influir en
intend to	pensar
interrupt	interrumpir
judge	juzgar

loathe	aborrecer
maintain	mantener
measure	medir
make a mistake (be wrong)	equivocarse
mistrust	desconfiar de, recelar
mix	mezclar
neglect	descuidar, desatender
notice	observar, notar
obey	obedecer
object to	oponerse a
offend	ofender
offer	ofrecer
omit	omitir
owe	deber
own	poseer, ser dueño de
permit	permitir
persuade to	persuadir a
possess	poseer
postpone	aplazar
prejudice	perjudicar
pretend (make believe)	fingir
prevent	impedir
profit from	aprovechar de
promise	prometer
propose	proponer
protect	proteger
prove	comprobar
provide	proveer, suministrar
quarrel	reñir
recognise	reconocer
refuse (to)	negarse (a), rehusar
regret (be sorry for)	sentir, lamentar
reject	rechazar
rely on	contar con, fiarse de
require	exigir
resemble	parecerse a
satisfy	satisfacer
scorn	desdeñar, despreciar
suit	convenir a
supply	suministrar
support	apoyar
suppose	suponer
suspect (of)	sospechar (de)
thank	agradecer
threaten (to / with)	amenazar (con + *inf* or *n*)
trust	fiarse de
waste (money / resources)	malgastar, despilfarrar
worry	inquietarse, preocuparse